LIGHTHOUSES SERIES

LIGHTHOUSES

of CALIFORNIA AND HAWAII

EUREKA *to* SAN DIEGO *to* HONOLULU

PHOTOGRAPHS *by* BRUCE ROBERTS
TEXT *by* RAY JONES

The Globe Pequot Press

GUILFORD, CONNECTICUT

Maritime beacons have marked key channels, harbors, and dangerous obstacles since the dawn of civilization. This rotating light atop the East Brother Lighthouse guides shipping in the upper San Francisco Bay.

Portions of this book previously appeared as *California Lighthouses.*

All photographs, unless otherwise credited, are by Bruce Roberts.
Text design by Nancy Freeborn
Map by M. A. Dubé

Library of Congress Cataloging-in-Publication Data
Jones, Ray, 1948–
        Lighthouses of California and Hawaii: Eureka to San Diego to Honolulu/
    photographs by Bruce Roberts; text by Ray Jones
            p.   cm. — (Lighthouses series)
        Includes bibliographical references.
        ISBN 0-7627-1219-8
        1. Lighthouses—California—Pictorial works. 2. Lighthouses—Hawaii—Pictorial works.
        I. Roberts, Bruce 1930– II. Title. III. Lighthouse series
    VK1024.C2 J6523 2002
    387.1'55'09794—dc21   2002067851

Front-cover photograph: East Brothers Light, California
Back-cver photograph: Point Vicente Light, California

Printed in Quebec, Canada
First Edition/First Printing

For BEN

—Ray Jones

For HERMAN JAEHNE,
who grew up at Point Reyes Light

—Bruce Roberts

The Old Point Loma Lighthouse dates from 1855.

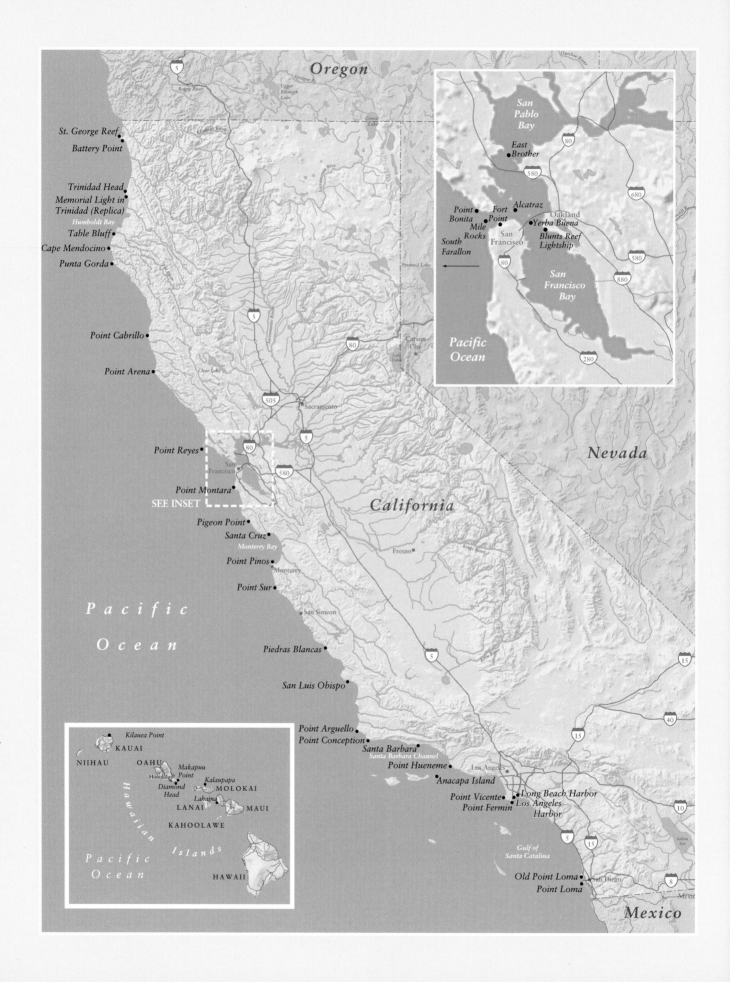

Oregon

St. George Reef
Battery Point

Trinidad Head
Memorial Light in
Trinidad (Replica)
Humboldt Bay
Table Bluff
Cape Mendocino
Punta Gorda

Point Cabrillo

Point Arena

Point Reyes

Point Montara
SEE INSET

Pigeon Point
Santa Cruz
Monterey Bay
Point Pinos
Monterey
Point Sur

San Simeon

Piedras Blancas

San Luis Obispo

Point Arguello
Point Conception
Santa Barbara
Santa Barbara Channel
Point Hueneme
Anacapa Island
Point Vicente
Point Fermin

Long Beach Harbor
Los Angeles
Harbor

Old Point Loma
Point Loma

*Pacific
Ocean*

California

Sacramento
Clear Lake
Lake Tahoe
Carson City ★

Fresno
Kings River
Kern River

Los Angeles

*Gulf of
Santa Catalina*

San Diego

Nevada

Mexico

Inset (upper right):

San
Pablo
Bay

East
Brother

Point
Bonita
Fort
Point
Mile
Rocks
South
Farallon
Alcatraz
Oakland
Yerba Buena
Blunts Reef
Lightship
San
Francisco

San
Francisco
Bay

*Pacific
Ocean*

Inset (lower left):

Kilauea Point
KAUAI
NIIHAU
OAHU
Makapuu
Point
Honolulu
Diamond
Head
Kalaupapa
MOLOKAI
Lahaina
LANAI
MAUI
KAHOOLAWE

Hawaiian Islands

*Pacific
Ocean*

HAWAII

CONTENTS

ACKNOWLEDGMENTS

*D*on and Carol Vestal at the Battery Point Lighthouse in Crescent City gave us a grand tour of the light tower and keeper's house even though it was in January and the lighthouse was officially closed. We will always remember seeing the St. George Reef Lighthouse in the distance. Afterward they turned on the Christmas lights for the last time this year so we could photograph them. Battery Point is known as the Christmas lighthouse since it was first lighted on Christmas Day 1856.

At Point Reyes Lighthouse Park Ranger Jim Kruse opened up the tower so we could get close-ups of the wonderful first-order Fresnel lens. Appreciation also goes to Dewey Livingston, historian at Point Reyes, for the information he has written in a Historic Structure Report for the National Park Service. A special thanks to all the volunteers at Point Arena Light who answered questions they hear a hundred times a day and helped with the photos in really cold weather. A special thanks to the park ranger at Point Bonita, whose name I lost, and to all the lighthouse volunteers who do long hours of standing and talking to the public at the California lights. It is because of these people that many of the lights are able to be open.

Thanks also to Nancy A. Pizzo of Pacific Highlights for her wonderful photos, particularly the picture of Battery Point Light at night. I'd also like to thank Bob and Sandra Shanklin, "The Lighthouse People," who have photographed every lighthouse in America that is still standing. Their photographs are priceless.

And thanks to Coast Guard Historian Robert Browning in Washington, D.C., for help in digging out old photos of lights long gone, to Jack Weil for his photos of lights still standing, and to Kim Andrews of Harbour Lights for her photo of Point Fermin after it was painted—it looks so much better with its new coat of paint.

And thanks to the U.S. Lighthouse Society in San Francisco for their wonderful "Photo Opportunities" list of California lights, which was helpful when I first photographed for the book in 1991. I hope their list and other material on California lights always remain available.

—*Bruce Roberts*

Many thanks to the United States Coast Guard for keeping the lights burning.

—*Ray Jones*

With its delightful Victorian architecture, the Point Fermin Lighthouse is now the centerpiece of a Los Angeles city park. Once dilapidated, the building was restored in 1974, its centennial year.

INTRODUCTION

Long before the United States had fifty states, the Spanish lit fires on Point Loma and elsewhere along the California coast to call their ships in from the sea. To mark channels and guide supply vessels to the mission and presidio at San Diego, they hung bright candles from poles. Otherwise the king's mariners were forced to navigate the dangerous California coast without the help of lights on the shore. Then came Mexican independence, Santa Anna, and the Mexican War with the United States. By the time the Treaty of Guadalupe Hidalgo ceded California to the United States in 1848, the old Spanish lights had flickered and gone dark.

The ink on the treaty was hardly dry before the discovery of gold in the Sierra foothills turned California from a remote possession into a passion for Americans. Suddenly, the Far West was seen as more than a place where formerly landless easterners carved out hardscrabble homesteads. It had a value that could be counted out in dollars, a lot of them. It offered not only cheap land and plenty of it but also the opportunity to get rich quick. The California gold rush was on.

Thousands of nearly trackless miles of wilderness separated the settled eastern states from the nation's newest and apparently richest seaboard. Obviously, most of the would-be millionaires who wanted to go to California and pan for gold would have to get there by ship. Just as obvious was the need for safe navigation on the West Coast. The nation could never hope to settle and exploit the West without a secure coastline, inviting to seaborne commerce.

GRAVEYARD OF THE PACIFIC

It had taken hundreds of years for European colonists to populate North America's East Coast. Even at this relatively leisurely pace, the settlement of the East had exacted a heavy toll. Thousands of ships were broken up by hurricanes, driven onto beaches and shattered by gales, or smashed by uncharted sandbars; uncounted thousands of sailors and passengers were drowned. The West was likely to be built up much faster than the East had been, and it was even less friendly to ships and sailors. Its shoreline stretched more than 2,000 rock-strewn miles, from Cape Flattery in the north to San Diego in the south.

Most maritime disasters happen, not on the open sea, but near the coast. For as long as ships have sailed the seas, sailors have paid with their lives when their vessels came too close to the shore. Destruction and death wait where the land meets water. Ships are built to withstand the stresses of high winds and giant waves, but a collision with rock, reef, or sand is usually fatal.

Unfortunately for many, such deadly encounters between ship and shore are common along the American West Coast. Stony capes jut out into the ocean like knife blades. Massive sea stacks rise up unexpectedly from the waves. Swift-running streams wash mud and gravel out of the mountains to form ship-killing shallows and block off the entrances of the rivers, where sea captains might otherwise find safe harbor from a storm.

The coastline of California is a geologically young and highly active continental margin. In some places mountains are rising out of the ocean, while in others they are sinking into it. Faults, volcanoes, and uplifts have raked and clawed these shores, leaving scores of rocky capes and points reaching far out into the sea. Sharp rocks and gravel-strewn sandbars lurk just beneath the waves. All this makes the coast a navigator's nightmare. And the weather compounds the mariner's problems. The prevailing winds and the powerful gales that sometimes accompany them blow out of the Pacific, driving vessels toward, not away from, the coast with its ship-killing rocks.

In the East, Cape Hatteras won dubious distinction as "the graveyard of the Atlantic." But the West has no maritime hazard comparable to Hatteras—at least none that stands out from the others. All of the West Coast is dangerous; all of it is a graveyard for ships and sailors, especially the California coast.

LIGHTING THE WEST

To help mariners navigate safely in the face of these dangers, Congress launched an ambitious construction program aimed at raising lighthouse towers at strategic locations all along the West Coast. Generally speaking, lighthouses perform two key services: They help pilots and navigators keep their ships on course, and they warn of impending calamity. The latter is, of course, their most vital and dramatic function. Lighthouses save ships, and they save lives.

With this in mind, government lighthouse officials hurried a survey team to the West in 1848. For months its members painstakingly navigated the wild and dangerous western shores. On more than one occasion the survey ships themselves came near disaster for lack of adequate charts and shore lights to guide their pilots. But the surveyors persevered, approaching treacherous headlands, sizing up dangerous rocks, sounding river channels, charting capes and points, noting likely construction sites, and even meeting with local Indian chiefs, perhaps to see if their tribes were hostile and likely to attack construction crews.

Before long the team had compiled a report recommending the establishment of a string of lighthouses reaching from Canada to Mexico. The report pointed to locations where the need for coastal markers was most critical—key harbors, important river entrances, threatening rocks and reefs. By 1852 Congress had narrowed down the survey list to sixteen sites where construction of lighthouses was to begin immediately. Included in the congressional authorization were Alcatraz Island, Fort Point, Point Bonita, and the Farallon Islands near San Francisco; Point Loma, Santa Barbara, Point Pinos, and Point Conception along the southern California coast; Humboldt Harbor and Crescent City in northern California; Cape Disappointment and the entrance of the Umpqua River in Oregon; and Cape Flattery, New Dungeness, Smith Island, and Willapa Bay (Cape Shoalwater) in Washington. Congress appropriated a total of $148,000 to launch the project, an impressive sum at the time, but one that would quickly prove woefully inadequate.

In an attempt to stretch these federal dollars as far as possible, government officials decided to hire a single contractor to build the first eight lights, seven of them in California and one in Oregon. Unfortunately, the savings that might have been realized through this approach never got beyond the door of the U.S. Treasury in Washington, D.C. Through a corrupt paper-shuffling scheme, the contract was let to an unscrupulous Treasury Department official who understood nothing whatsoever about the construction of lighthouses. He had no intention, however, of building them himself. He quickly sold the contract to a Baltimore firm, reaping a handsome profit in the process.

The company that ended up with the contract was a partnership consisting of Francis Kelly and Francis Gibbons. The latter was a veteran lighthouse engineer who had built the Bodie Island Lighthouse on the Outer Banks of North Carolina. With their contract in hand, Kelly and Gibbons loaded up the sailing ship *Oriole* with nails, lumber, and supplies and sent it off to California by way of storm-lashed Cape Horn.

When the *Oriole* arrived at San Francisco late in 1852, Gibbons's construction crew began work immediately on the Alcatraz Island Lighthouse. Gibbons believed he and his men could build several lighthouses at once and that the work could be done faster and more efficiently in stages. So once the foundation was finished on Alcatraz, he moved part of his crew to Fort Point, where they

Built in 1854 on San Francisco Bay's Alcatraz Island, this veteran of the gold rush is California's first true lighthouse, shown here as it looked during the Civil War. Note the long rows of stacked cannonballs. (Courtesy National Archives)

prepared the site and started laying a second foundation. Hopping from place to place in this way, Gibbons's workers had four lighthouses standing within ten months. Then disaster struck.

In August 1853 the *Oriole* set sail from San Francisco to the mouth of the Columbia River, where work was scheduled to begin on a fifth lighthouse at Cape Disappointment. Having no light to guide her, the ship struck shoals near the entrance of the river and began to take on water. Feverish efforts to save the vessel proved unsuccessful, and she sank, carrying all the remaining construction materials down with her. Fortunately, the ship's crew and its complement of lighthouse builders were rescued.

Gibbons and Kelly scrambled frantically to replace the lost materials. Within a few months the partners had commissioned another ship and stocked her with supplies so that work could resume. By redoubling their efforts and working on several sites at once, they were able to get the project back on schedule. In August 1854, one year after the sinking of the *Oriole,* the last brick was laid on the Point Loma Lighthouse. All eight of the contracted lighthouses were now complete.

LIGHT FROM PARIS

Ironically, although eight lighthouse towers now stood along the West Coast, only two were able to display a light. The recently established Lighthouse Board in Washington had decided to equip the new lighthouses with advanced Fresnel lenses, which were manufactured in Paris. The prisms of such lenses (many of them survive to this day) were designed to gather every available flicker from a light source and bend it into a horizontal plane. Thus concentrated and directed, the light could

Many of California's early lighthouses were modest structures. This combination residence and tower on Point Loma near San Diego was built of locally quarried sandstone during the 1850s.

often be seen from dozens of miles away. Some of the lenses were also given bull's-eyes, which focused the light and caused it to flash intermittently.

Although a Fresnel lens looks like a single piece of molded glass, it is not. The lens consists of individual prisms—sometimes more than a thousand of them—fitted into a metal frame. This makes them look like giant glass beehives. It also makes them rather delicate.

Fresnels come in a variety of sizes, referred to as "orders." The huge first-order lenses, such as the one that once nearly filled the lantern room of the St. George's Reef Lighthouse, in northern California, are six feet in diameter and as much as ten feet tall. The smallest lenses, designated sixth order, are only one foot in diameter.

The one drawback of Fresnel-type lenses—and it is a considerable one—is that they require a lot of care. They must be cleaned and polished frequently by hand, and the mechanisms that turn flashing Fresnels are large and cumbersome. As a consequence, the Coast Guard has replaced many of the old Fresnels with airport-type beacons, which are easier to maintain.

On those rare and unfortunate occasions when Fresnel lenses are severely damaged or destroyed by storms or vandalism, they cannot be replaced. The expense would be prohibitive, perhaps running into the millions of dollars. The original lenses were hand ground and hand polished by the poorest classes of French laborers, including Parisian children, who worked for pennies a day. It is ironic that the handiwork of these unhappy and unremembered workers is numbered among the most durable and practical devices ever made. No one will ever know how many lives have been saved by Fresnel lenses, how many accidents did not happen because light was there on the horizon, offering warning and guidance to sailors. Once completed, these expensive lenses had to be carefully packed and shipped more than 12,000 miles around the tip of South America's Cape Horn to reach California. The West's first Fresnels—a matched pair of third-order lenses—came in the fall of 1853 and were installed in the tower at Alcatraz Island and at Point Pinos near Monterey. By spring the Alcatraz lens was in place. On June 1, 1854, the keeper lit the lamp inside the sparkling lens and a sheet of light reached out across the dark waters of San Francisco Bay, ushering in a new and safer era of navigation in the West.

Although rightfully proud of their accomplishments, Gibbons and Kelly were in for a shock. So were government inspectors and lighthouse officials. When the next shipment of lenses arrived from Paris, they would not fit in the lanterns atop the towers of any of the light-houses. The lanterns and, in some cases, the towers themselves were too small to accommodate the big prismatic lenses. Every light-house had to be renovated, and the towers at Point Conception and on the Farallon Islands had to be torn down and completely re-built. Gibbons and Kelly had contracted to build the lighthouses for $15,000 each. The cost of renovations and rebuilding, added to the cost incurred from the tragic loss of the *Oriole,* doubtless more than wiped out any profit the Baltimore businessmen had hoped to reap on the project.

At night a giant bull's-eye lens focuses Point Arena's first-order beacon. The light is supplied by one of the high-intensity bulbs shown here. The second bulb is a spare.

The remaining eight lighthouses authorized by Congress in 1852 were built by other contractors. Most were under construction by the mid-1850s, and the final two, the Willapa Bay and Smith Island lighthouses in Washington, were completed and in operation by October 1858. By that time sixteen lights shone out toward the sea from their appointed locations along the West Coast.

Many of these first western lighthouses were built following a single basic architectural scheme, that of a Cape Cod–style dwelling with the tower thrusting up through the center of the roof. This design offered the obvious advantage of allowing the keeper to service the light without braving the damp and chilly coastal weather. But the Cape Cod style seemed out of place in the West, especially in California, where Spanish-style architecture was dominant. Later western lighthouses reverted to a more traditional design featuring a conical or octagonal freestanding tower, beside which was constructed an accompanying frame dwelling.

LIGHTHOUSES IN PARADISE

California had been a state for almost half a century by the time Hawaii and its sea lanes became a responsibility of the U.S. government. Its monarchy overthrown by wealthy planters in 1894, Hawaii was annexed by the United States just four years later. Not long afterward, Congress appropriated funds for the construction of lighthouses on Oahu and other islands in the Hawaiian chain.

These navigational lights were definitely needed, for while the remote, mid-Pacific islands were almost entirely dependent on the ocean, they presented mariners with a unique challenge. The rolling Pacific linked the islands to one another, and until the 1930s, when air service became available, all travel between them had to be accomplished by water. The ocean also linked Hawaii with the outside world, and its prosperous plantation economy could never have survived without the ships that carried its sugar and pineapple to market.

Little more than specks on a mariner's chart, the islands were all but lost in the vast, blue of the Pacific. Finding them demanded every ounce of talent a navigator could muster—and sometimes more—but even local navigation in Hawaiian waters could be difficult and dangerous. Offering few sheltered harbors, Hawaii threatened vessels large and small with towering seawalls, jagged volcanic rocks, and tricky currents.

To guide mariners to safety, a necklace of sparkling navigational lights was constructed to circle the islands. Among the most unusual and powerful beacons in America, Hawaii's lighthouses were built on old lava flows or on the slopes of ancient volcanoes. Completed in 1899, the Diamond Head tower west of Honolulu gripped a scorched volcanic crater known locally as the "Ring of Fire." Built in 1908 atop a jumble of volcanic rocks, the soaring Kalaupapa tower shared a remote Molokai peninsula with a notorious leper colony. Raised in 1909 on a site blasted from a cliff of lava, Oahu's Makapuu Point tower was fitted with a giant Fresnel lens more than 12 feet high and weighing several tons. These and several other extraordinary Hawaiian lighthouses remain in operation to this day and must be counted among the exotic treasures of America's fiftieth state.

A NAVIGATIONAL TRADITION

Eventually, major coastal and primary harbor lights guided ships along the nation's western shores. Not all are still standing, and more than a few have been taken out of service and allowed to go dark. But a surprising number of the old lighthouses have survived, in some cases for more than a century, the ravages of earthquake, wind, and weather. Many of the old lights are still burning, offering guidance to any sailor on the sea. Even today, none but the most foolish mariner would ignore their warnings.

This book tells a part—admittedly a small part—of the story of California's and Hawaii's lighthouses. Through words and pictures, it gives the reader a look at these unique structures as well as a glimpse at their fascinating histories. Each, as you'll see, has its own rich story to tell. The book can also be used as a guide to the lights. General directions and travel information are provided for each of the lighthouses. Some of the lights, though inaccessible, can still be seen from nearby vantage points, directions to which are also included.

Each chapter opens with a visit to one or more of its region's most dramatic and inaccessible lighthouses. Building them required extraordinary ingenuity, courage, and strength. Servicing them demanded the best their keepers could give—sometimes all they could give and more. Each in its own way is a symbol, the distilled essence of a noble navigational tradition reaching back to the beginnings of civilization.

The Battery Point Lighthouse near Crescent City sends its beacon out over the Pacific just as it has done since 1856. (Courtesy Nancy A. Pizzo)

Completed in 1892, the St. George Reef Lighthouse represented an almost miraculous feat of engineering and construction. This late nineteenth-century photograph shows a U.S. Lighthouse Service crew approaching the station. (Courtesy National Archives)

CHAPTER ONE

LIGHTS OF THE REDWOOD COAST

Northern California

ome commercial fishermen still call it the Dragon. In 1792 English explorer George Vancouver gave this deadly reef the name Dragon Rocks. The name was later changed to St. George Reef. But whether medieval saint or dragon, the reef is a legend among mariners. Most consider it a monster.

St. George Reef is the peak of a submerged volcanic mountain about six miles off the extreme north coast of California. Its uppermost rocks reach just above the toss of the waves, out of sight to all but the sharpest-eyed sailor. The rocks rise abruptly from the sea, and there are no surrounding shallows to warn ships that they are approaching disaster. During rough weather, waves breaking over the rocks throw an obscuring blanket of mist over the reef, making it practically invisible.

ST. GEORGE AND THE DRAGON

For the passengers and crew of the Civil War–era side-wheel steamer *Brother Jonathan,* the reef was a sea monster indeed—a merciless one. Plowing through heavy weather on the way to San Francisco, the *Brother Jonathan* slammed into the reef and sank in a matter of minutes. Nearly 200 lives were lost in the calamity.

The tragic loss of the *Brother Jonathan* became something of a scandal. Why had nothing been done to mark this obvious and death-dealing maritime hazard? The *Brother Jonathan* was not the only vessel to open its hull on the reef's sharp rocks, and there had been many other deaths. A cemetery in Crescent City was filled with the graves of mariners who would have lived longer had it not been for St. George Reef. Sailors, maritime interests, and the general public demanded action.

It was not immediately clear to the Lighthouse Board what should be done, however. If a lighthouse were built, should it—or could it—be placed on the rocks themselves? Building the lighthouse directly over the reef would require an Olympian feat of engineering and construction and might be prohibitively expensive. A plan to build a mainland lighthouse on nearby St. George Point had to be abandoned because the site was shown to be too far from the reef to serve as an effective warning. Most vessels navigating this area made it a practice to run well offshore, and many of them could not see the light if its source were on the mainland.

So, after much debate, the board decided to shoulder the task of building a light tower on the exposed, wave-swept rocks of St. George Reef. To execute the daunting project, the board hired M. A. Ballantyne, who had led the conquest of Tillamook Rock only the year before. With the Tillamook Lighthouse complete—a construction project many had thought impossible—and its light burning, Ballantyne brought his crew of experienced workers south during the winter of 1882.

Aboard the 126-ton schooner *LaNinfa,* Ballantyne and his crew anchored off St. George Reef for several weeks. Weather conditions were so rough that Ballantyne's surveyors and workers managed to get onto the rocks only three times in a stretch of four weeks. But by the early spring, work was under way. Ballantyne's formidable crew of nearly fifty workmen rigged a cable from the rock's highest point—about fifty-four feet—to the schooner, which had been secured with heavy mooring tackle.

Like a tall ship slicing through a pounding sea, the St. George Lighthouse stands up to the Pacific. Constantly manned for more than eighty years, the lighthouse served from 1892 until 1972, when the Coast Guard abandoned the site. (Courtesy U.S. Coast Guard)

The cable served as an aerial tramway, allowing workers to slide to the rock in a breeches buoy, a life ring with canvas pants attached to the cable. Tools and equipment were transferred to the rock inside a stout cage. A small derrick and hoist on the rock helped pull the men and equipment up the tramway to the construction site, while gravity provided the power for the return trip to *LaNinfa*.

As they became used to riding over the sea, the workers started using the open cage to make trips to and from the rock. As many as six men could ride in the cage at a time, and this made it possible to evacuate the work site in a matter of minutes when dangerous storms swept in off the Pacific. While his men carved the foundation and built the inverted pyramidal base on which the light tower would stand, Ballantyne kept an eye on the seaward horizon. When swells began to build and a storm threatened, he would give the alarm and send his men gliding back over the tramway in the cage to the relative safety of *LaNinfa*.

The sea was not the only danger faced by the builders. The glycerine powder used for blasting out the foundation was highly unstable, and an accidental explosion was always a threat. What is more, the hard but brittle stone of the reef shattered easily, and the crew was often showered with sharp, shrapnel-like rock fragments when the glycerine was detonated. When blasting, the workers scurried for cover like infantrymen under attack. Despite precautions, there were frequent injuries, and even *LaNinfa* was sometimes hit by blast fragments.

The work did not progress as smoothly or steadily as it had at Tillamook. Furious storms and long stretches of generally horrible weather produced long delays. So, too, did lack of money. The original congressional appropriation had been highly unrealistic, and soon bills began to stack up faster than the stones of the light tower. Not until 1887 did Congress provide sufficient funds for the structure to be completed. Eventually the government spent a whopping $704,633 on the project, making this the most expensive lighthouse in the nation's history.

As work continued, a seventy-foot-high reinforced concrete pier was firmly anchored to the rock. Once the pier was finished, it became the base for a granite tower consisting of 1,339 blocks of dressed stone. The tower's heaviest blocks weighed up to two and a half tons each. The huge stones were cut and fit together with such precision that they had no more than a $\frac{3}{16}$-inch gap between them. Hefty metal dowels held the big stones one to another. Cement and cut stone were forced into even the smallest openings between the granite stones so that the completed tower was like a solid piece of rock.

The St. George Reef Lighthouse was at last placed in service on October 20, 1892, more than ten years after construction got under way. The station's first-order Fresnel lens shined from atop a 134-foot, square-shaped tower with a circular stairwell leading up one side to the lantern room. The keepers gained access to the stairway by passing through the boiler, coal, and laundry rooms at the base. As they climbed, they passed successive levels containing a galley, the head keeper's quarters, the assistant keepers' quarters, the watch room (later the radio room), and finally the lantern room with its enormous lens.

The station was considered too isolated and dangerous for families, so most lighthouse personnel maintained homes on the mainland. The government provided residences for families on St. George Point. The station crew consisted of five men who worked four weeks on and two weeks off. The long unrelieved stretches of work created tension between members of the station crew. On one occasion, during a month-long series of fierce storms that prevented relief personnel from reaching the rock, crew members stopped talking to one another altogether. At mealtimes they sat facing away from the table so they would not have to look at one another.

Eventually the crewmen settled their argument, but no one at Dragon Rock ever made complete peace with the sea. St. George Lighthouse developed a reputation as one of the most dangerous light stations in America. On several occasions crewmen were killed while traveling to or from the reef. In 1951 three coastguardsmen were drowned in a single incident when waves swamped the station launch.

Vancouver, the explorer who gave the reef the name Dragon Rocks, also named the nearby point after the mythical dragon slayer St. George. Perhaps he meant the names as a joke. But the dragon reef is no joke, and unlike St. George's dragon, it has never been conquered. In 1972 the Coast Guard abandoned the St. George Lighthouse and replaced it with a buoy. The reef was then left unwatched and untrammeled by humans, to carry on its ageless battle with the sea.

The big lens that once crowned the St. George Lighthouse was a Fresnel, a type first made in Paris early in the nineteenth century. Many of the old lighthouses along the West Coast still depend on their original Fresnel lenses to focus the light that mariners and more than a few delighted landlubbers see glimmering from a distance. Surprisingly, the older lenses—some of them made more than 150 years ago—are often as good as, or better than, those manufactured today. "The Fresnels can still be used because this technology reached its zenith more than a century ago," says one coastguardsman. "There have been very few improvements since the 1850s."

BATTERY POINT LIGHT

Crescent City – 1856

Now a museum, the Battery Point Light once helped fuel the economy of this community situated on the far north coast of California. During the nineteenth century big trees, most of them redwoods, made the place a boomtown. The ancient trees were being cut down to build San Francisco, and the lumber was loaded onto ships in the Crescent City harbor. The lighthouse guided the lumber ships in and out and warned them of dangerous rocks near the harbor entrance.

The citizens of Crescent City were among the first in California to petition the government for a lighthouse. In 1855 Congress appropriated $15,000 to purchase a tract of land and build the station. A brick tower and stone keeper's cottage were built on rocks at the end of Battery Point, about forty-five feet above the sea. As with many early California lighthouses, the tower rose through the center of the dwelling. Atop the fifty-foot tower a fourth-order Fresnel lens beamed seaward.

The station's first official keeper was Theophilus Magruder, who arrived with his wife at Battery Point on Christmas Day in 1856. A native of Washington, D.C., Magruder had led a sophisticated social life before he left the East to search for gold in Oregon. Along with his partner, James Marshall, Magruder combed the Oregon coastal mountains and panned its streams for years, never finding the precious metal he sought. Eventually the pair split up, and Marshall drifted off to the Sierra foothills, where he not only found gold but touched off the great California gold rush of 1849.

First lit in December 1856, the Battery Point Lighthouse is known to most in Crescent City as "the Christmas Light." The resident museum keepers decorate the old building with strings of colored lights each December.

Magruder also found glitter, although not of the golden variety, by tending a gleaming new Fresnel lens at the Battery Point Lighthouse. When he could spare the time, Magruder relaxed in a chair built for him by his old partner and, no doubt, dreamed of what his life might have been like had he struck gold instead of Marshall.

Captain John Jeffrey took over keeper's duties at the Battery Point Lighthouse in 1875. He and his wife, Nellie, became fixtures of the station, almost as durable as the thick stone walls of the lighthouse itself. In all, they spent thirty-nine years at the station and raised four children there.

Life at the station was not without its trials. The Jeffrey children had to scramble across a low-water causeway on their way to school. Sometimes they were trapped on the mainland by high tide and could not get home. On such occasions Captain Jeffrey came for them in the station boat.

Because of its exposed location, the lighthouse took a beating when storms rolled in off the Pacific. Often water poured through the doors and windows and even down the chimney. The Jeffreys barely escaped tragedy in 1879 when a huge wave dislodged the wall of their kitchen and knocked over a lighted stove. Flames engulfed the kitchen, and the family would have been forced to abandon the dwelling along with all their possessions had not a second wave washed over the house and put out the blaze.

On occasion, the waves that hit the lighthouse were so large that they cracked the windows in the lantern room. Despite the regular pounding, however, the old building survived for decade after decade.

Except for a stroke of luck, the station's last night might have been that of March 27, 1964. The earthquake that hit Alaska on that date sent five titanic tidal waves hurtling toward the coast of northern California, where they stormed ashore shortly after midnight. Keepers Clarence and Peggy Coons saw them coming but could do little more than say their prayers. Fortunately, the enormous waves struck at such an extreme angle that the lighthouse was spared. Crescent City itself, however, was not so lucky. The walls of water destroyed multistory buildings, crushed houses, and washed cars and trucks into the sea. In all, twenty-nine city blocks were demolished. But through it all, the Battery Point Light kept flashing.

As resident curators of the Battery Point Lighthouse Museum, Don and Carol Vestal live much like the generations of hardy keepers who came before them.

As a museum maintained by the Del Norte County Historical Society, the lighthouse appears today much as it did when its lamp was first lit in 1856. It serves as a major maritime attraction and is even reputed to harbor a ghost. At least six people are said to have heard the ghost's seabooted feet slowly climbing the tower steps during severe storms.

Even if they do not meet up with the ghost, visitors will find plenty to see here. In addition to an array of early lighthouse equipment, the edifice displays artifacts from some of the less fortunate vessels that did not reach the safety of the harbor. In the main room is a bell from the steamer *Brother Jonathan*, which sank off Battery Point with a loss of 200 lives. Also on display are a number of items salvaged from the World War II tanker *Emidio*, a victim of torpedoes fired by a Japanese submarine lurking off the California coast.

HOW TO GET THERE: *The Del Norte County Historical Society maintains the lighthouse as a history museum. The lighthouse stands on the west side of the harbor on Battery Point. The light shines nightly through a drum-type lens. Hours are Wednesday through Sunday 10:00 A.M. to 5:00 P.M.—when the tide is out. For more information call (707) 464–3089 or write to the society at 577 H Street, Crescent City, CA 95531.*

TRINIDAD HEAD LIGHT
Trinidad – 1871

Set back from a jagged cliff face 196 feet above the Pacific surf, the Trinidad Head Lighthouse has aided commercial fishermen returning to the safety of the port of Trinidad for more than a century. Trinidad Harbor nestles behind a broad headland, which absorbs most of the fury of the ocean's winter storms. Some of them are ferocious indeed.

One of the largest storm waves ever recorded struck Trinidad Head on December 31, 1914. It was observed by keeper Fred Harrington, and had the wave been only a little more powerful, neither the lighthouse nor Harrington would have survived it.

For more than an hour Harrington had watched the gale grow ever stronger in force, and he could see enormous waves breaking over the top of 103-foot Pilot Rock about half a mile to the south. As the keeper turned to wipe moisture from the lantern windows, he saw a mountainous sea sweeping toward the headland and the lighthouse. For a moment he stood watching in horror, but there was nothing he could do but hope for the best. Seconds later the huge wave hit the rocks, throwing a wall of green water over the lighthouse.

Windows were broken and the mechanism that rotated the light was stopped, but when the water rushed back down into the sea, the lighthouse and Harrington were still standing. The keeper had the light flashing again in fewer than thirty minutes.

Yurok Indians were the first people known to have ventured seaward from the sheltered cove behind Trinidad Head. In the summer of 1775 the Spanish explorers Heceta and Bodega arrived to survey Humboldt Bay. By 1854 American settlements had been established, and residents petitioned Congress for a lighthouse to guide lumber boats in and out of the harbor.

No work was done for nearly two decades, however, as California's coastal communities jostled one another in competition for scarce federal funds. It would be almost fifteen years before lighthouse officials took note of the little fishing, logging, and mining community of Trinidad. By the 1870s Trinidad's harbor was attracting regular schooner traffic from San Francisco and shipping loads of lumber to help build up the new western metropolis.

In the spring of 1871 workmen carved out a shelf from the rock and started building the twenty-five-foot brick tower. The oil lamp inside the station's fourth-order Fresnel lens was first lit on December 1, 1871.

The new light helped close a gap of darkness between Crescent City in the north and Humboldt Bay to the south. While the station's fourth-order lens was small for a coastal light, the elevation of the tower, which was perched on a high cliff, made its beacon visible from up to 20 miles at sea. The light's first keeper was a man named Jeremiah Kiler. While he had no previous experience with lighthouses, he served efficiently for more than seventeen years.

An enormous fog bell was placed on the head in 1898. The bell was so loud that its vibrations soon shook loose the weights that helped ring it, and, together with their cables, they plunged into the sea. The bell proved too strong for the replacement mechanism as well. It is easy to imagine what it did to the keeper's ears.

Today, the Trinidad Head Lighthouse is automated and closed to the public. Because it is located on the opposite side of the headland, it cannot be seen from the town. Hiking trails lead to an overlook with a view of the old lighthouse, but less energetic visitors have another attractive option.

For the benefit of tourists who constantly ask the locals how to get to the lighthouse, a replica of the tower has been built in the town. It is a near-perfect match and even houses one component of the original. When Trinidad Head station was automated in 1947, its Fresnel lens was replaced by an airport-style beacon. A local organization later acquired the antique lens, and it now graces the replica of the tower.

HOW TO GET THERE: *Off Highway 101 about 20 miles north of Eureka, the town of Trinidad has two almost identical lighthouses, the original one, on Trinidad Head, and the replica built nearer the road for the benefit of visitors. The tourist lighthouse contains the Fresnel lens that once graced the old light tower on the head.*

A replica of the Trinidad Head Lighthouse overlooks the rock-strewn northern California shore. Nearby is the quaint village of Trinidad Head, where visitors can still buy fresh salmon from local fishermen.

LIGHTHOUSES OF HUMBOLDT HARBOR

Humboldt Bay – **1856**
Table Bluff – **1892**

Completed in 1856, at a time when much of the U.S. Pacific coast was still a wilderness, the Humboldt Harbor Lighthouse was among the first light stations in the West. Built at a cost of $15,000, the lighthouse consisted of a Cape Cod–style dwelling with a twenty-one-foot tower rising through the middle section of its roof. The lantern room held a fourth-order Fresnel lens.

Built on a sandy foundation, the lighthouse was threatened by nature almost from the beginning. Wracked by earthquakes, storms, and beach erosion, the structure began to deteriorate. In 1885 a mighty cyclone tore away its roof and drove floating logs against its walls. The building was repaired, but it was

never the same again. The walls of both the tower and the dwelling began to crack, and lighthouse officials soon became convinced that the old lighthouse was unsalvageable.

By 1892 a new lighthouse high atop nearby Table Bluff was ready for service. A Victorian-style structure with an attached square tower, it was given the same fourth-order lens that had once shone from the tower of the harbor lighthouse. Although the Table Bluff tower was only thirty-five feet tall, its elevation placed the light almost 190 feet above the bay. The light could be seen from up to twenty miles away.

For many years, the old Humboldt Harbor Lighthouse was used as a dwelling for various government employees or service personnel, but its deterioration continued. Eventually, it was abandoned altogether. In a storm during the 1930s, it finally collapsed into a jumble of masonry on the beach.

In time, the Table Bluff Lighthouse would also be threatened with destruction. Automated during the 1950s, it was decommissioned in 1975 and turned over to a private foundation. Neglected and in disrepair, it might have been torn down had not a group of energetic volunteers stepped in to save it. The tower of the lighthouse was cut into two parts and trucked away to Woodley Island near Eureka. There it was reassembled, repaired, and refitted with the station's old Fresnel lens. Today it serves as a tourist attraction and a reminder of the area's rich maritime history.

HOW TO GET THERE: *Nothing remains of the old Humboldt Harbor Light except, perhaps, a few chunks of stone on the beach. The Table Bluff Light tower, however, remains in excellent condition and is on display at Woodley Island in the Eureka Inner Harbor area. To reach Woodley Island, take Highway 101 into Eureka, turn toward the water on Highway 255, and follow signs to the lighthouse. The nearby Humboldt Bay Maritime Museum is also well worth a visit. For hours and other information, call (707) 444–9440.*

Table Bluff Light (Courtesy Bob and Sandra Shanklin)

CAPE MENDOCINO LIGHT
Shelter Cove – 1868

You can't go much farther west in the West than Cape Mendocino—it is the westernmost point in California. Towering 1,400 feet above the ocean and dropping almost vertically down to it, the cape is the highest headland in California. It is also one of the wildest, windiest, and most beautiful.

In the spring wildflowers spangle the cape's rolling, grassy hills. Narrow forests of tall trees struggle for footholds in ravines, where they find protection from the nearly constant winds. Often the wind can be heard whistling over and around Sugar Loaf, a 326-foot rock about 250 yards offshore.

The weather at Cape Mendocino is fickle, shifting quickly from fog to gale to sunshine and back to fog all in a single afternoon. The changes come with little or no warning. The contrariness of the weather here is due to a climatic peculiarity. The chilly northern current that drives the weather of northern California makes a sudden change of course off the cape, causing warm and cool air masses to mix, with unpredictable results.

During the 1500s Spanish galleons returning to Mexico from the Philippines used the cape to determine their position. Intending to keep well away from the cape and its perilous rock, they turned south here, making for Acapulco. Lost in fog or driven onward by the wind, more than a few turned too late and ended their days as rotting hulks on the cape's beaches.

Nowadays, sailors are warned of the cape's dangers by an automated light shining seaward from atop a polelike structure some 515 feet up the cape's west-facing slope. The old lighthouse, which handled the same job faithfully for more than a century, has been moved to the town of Shelter Cove just south of the cape.

Although only forty-seven feet tall, the lighthouse was located 422 feet above the sea, which made it one of the highest marine-navigation lights in the United States.

The need for the light was dramatized on January 4, 1860, when the Pacific mail steamer *Northerner*, bound from San Francisco to the Columbia River, crashed on Two Fathoms Rock only a mile from the proposed light station. The steamer took thirty-eight passengers and crew down with her.

To build the lighthouse, crews had to carve terraces from the slope. Materials were brought ashore through the surf from a lighthouse tender and hauled up a steep, winding trail.

Once completed, the lighthouse and dwellings were far from comfortable. Fierce winter winds blew down chimneys, shattered windows, and shook the very walls. During a particularly violent storm, one assistant keeper was forced to flee his residence and take refuge in the more solidly built lighthouse tower. Another had his house almost blown apart in a storm and afterward moved his family into the station's smelly oil house.

The Cape Mendocino Lighthouse looks like an empty bird cage without its huge, first-order Fresnel lens, removed when the station was automated in 1950. Abandoned during the 1970s, the old tower clung to its 380-foot promontory until 1998 when it was moved to the nearby Shelter Cover for display in a park. (Courtesy Bob and Sandra Shanklin)

The wind made walking back and forth between the residences and lighthouse a perilous adventure. Even the most surefooted keepers had to watch their step or run the risk of being blown off the cliff. A sleeping shanty was attached to the tower so keepers could avoid these hazards when gales were howling.

HOW TO GET THERE: *The original Cape Mendicino Light tower is located in Mal Coombs Park in the town of Shelter Cove. It can be reached by way of a winding mountain road off U.S. Highway 101 near Redway.*

The Cape Mendocino Lighthouse during its active-duty years when it was carefully maintained by resident keepers. The pole on the left is a radio beacon tower. (Courtesy U.S. Coast Guard)

PUNTA GORDA LIGHT

Petrolia – 1912

Located on one of the loneliest, least accessible stretches of northern California's famed Redwood Coast, Punta Gorda Lighthouse was as difficult to maintain as it was to build. For this reason the Coast Guard abandoned the light as soon as it became practical to do so. Established in 1912, the station was closed permanently in 1951. All that remains of it today is a single-story concrete watch room with a spiral staircase leading up to an iron lantern room overhead. Resting on a bluff forty-eight feet above the surf, the entire structure stands only twenty-seven feet high.

The little lighthouse now seems a natural part of the pristine landscape in which it was built. The area is a delight for hardy hikers. Plants cascade down the steep bluffs to beaches populated primarily by seals and pelicans. During the 1960s the government had the station's wooden buildings burned to discourage squatters.

Punta Gorda is a rounded, nearly treeless cape rising 800 feet above the sea. A spur of high ground called Windy Point runs seaward from the cape, creating a hazard for ships. Before the era of electronic navigation, the overhanging mountains made it nearly impossible for sailors to take a bearing on Punta Gorda, especially on dark nights. Eight ships were lost near Punta Gorda between 1899 and 1907. The last of these, the *Columbia*, took eighty-seven people down with her.

Prompted by these disasters, Congress took action in 1908, appropriating funds to buy land and establish a light station. But building the new lighthouse was not easy. Materials had to be landed well to the north of the site and then dragged down the beach on horse-drawn sleds. Nonetheless, construction crews managed to erect not only the lighthouse but also three large dwellings, a blacksmith and carpentry shop, an oil house, three storage sheds, and a water and sewage system. By 1911 the station fog signal had begun to sound; early the next year the tower's fourth-order Fresnel lens began to cast its flashing light toward the sea.

Since there were no roads, keepers used horse-drawn wagons to bring supplies along the beaches from Petrolia, about eleven miles away. Picking up the mail required a long ride on horseback. Almost until the time the station closed, keepers and their families used horses and mules for transportation.

But despite their isolation, Punta Gorda keepers lived and ate well. There were plenty of deer for venison, an abundance of trout in nearby Fourmile Creek, all the abalone anyone could ever eat in the sea, and, in the summer, a heaven of wild blackberries.

HOW TO GET THERE: *From Highway 101 in northern California, take the Cape Mendocino Road from Fortuna and follow it to the village of Petrolia. Park near the trail to the coast and the lighthouse, and brace yourself for a 3½-mile hike. Dress warmly, since this part of the California coast can be chilly, even during the summer. Not much is left of the old station, but it can be a haunting place to visit. The remains of wrecked ships can be seen near the abandoned lighthouse.*

Punta Gorda Light (Courtesy Bob and Sandra Shanklin)

POINT CABRILLO LIGHT

Mendocino – 1909

When the sea is running, it slams against Point Cabrillo, hurling spray onto rocks near the top of the sixty-foot cliffs. A salty mist settles on wildflowers and the needles of cypress hedgerows that line the headland, while down below seawater rushes into a honeycomb of tunnels reaching far back under the point. Some of these tunnels cut directly beneath the Point Cabrillo Lighthouse, but for the moment, at least, the ground under the station remains solid.

The point is blanketed by fog for an average of 1,000 hours a year, but often the weather is clear and the sun bright. The lighthouse was automated in the 1970s, but during the more than six decades it was manned, the good weather, rich soil, and abundant fresh water made it easy for lighthouse keepers to raise food and feed their families. Usually, they tilled large gardens and kept cows, pigs, and chickens. Easy access to schools, churches, and stores, along with its lovely pastoral setting, helped make Point Cabrillo a popular duty station.

The lighthouse itself adds to the bucolic feeling of the place. Its steeplelike tower gives it the look of a small country church. Despite its appearance, this is a hard-working yeoman of a lighthouse with more than eighty years of service to mariners. The lamp at the top of the forty-seven-foot tower was first lit on June 10, 1909. Its third-order Fresnel lens was mounted on four tiers of brass pillars, and it rotated on chariot wheels with heavy ball bearings.

It was the lumber industry that petitioned the gov-

The Point Cabrillo Lighthouse has the bucolic appearance of an old country church or a schoolhouse. Its beacon first served mariners in 1909. (Courtesy Nancy A. Pizzo)

ernment to build the Point Cabrillo Lighthouse, so it is perhaps not surprising that all of the station's buildings were made of wood. With the tower rising from its roof, the main structure suggests the Cape Cod style of California's earliest lighthouses. Painted white with gray trim, it was given a red roof and black lantern.

The largest portion of the building once housed the big gas engines and air compressors that powered the station's two fog signals. Facing seaward, the horns protruded through the roof of the building. They resembled the trumpet-shaped exhausts of belowdecks ventilators on ships. During the 1980s the foghorns were removed, and a sound buoy took over their task of warning sailors away from the point's dangerous rocks. Many ships have been lost along this treacherous stretch of coast, more than a few of them schooners and freighters carrying lumber harvested from the area's once-dense forests. These slow-moving vessels were particularly vulnerable to storms that

howled out of the north and east without warning. Unwary crews often found themselves driven onto the rocks.

In February 1960 one such storm almost carried away the lighthouse itself. It was a gale of such violence that two-ton boulders were torn away from the cliff face and thrown shoreward. Enormous waves surged up the sides of the cliff and swept over the grass, slamming into the heavy doors at the seaward end of the building. Soon the doors caved in, and a huge generator was ripped from its floor bolts and shoved against the far wall. When the sea retreated the following day, it left a foot of gravel and sand on the floor.

HOW TO GET THERE: *Located off California Route 1 near Mendocino, the Point Cabrillo Light station is being restored for use as a museum. Contact the North Coast Interpretive Association, Box 641, Mendocino, CA 95420; (707) 937–0816.*

An early twentieth-century view of the Point Cabrillo Lighthouse. Notice the twin fog-signal horns protruding from the roof. (Courtesy U.S. Coast Guard)

POINT ARENA LIGHT

Point Arena – 1870 AND 1908

Motorists driving along California Route 1 north of San Francisco are struck by the gentle appearance of the landscape. They see green fields running right down to the edge of the blue Pacific and small herds of contented cattle and sheep grazing in rich pastures covered by thick carpets of grass. The rugged mountains just to the east form a wall that seems to protect this pastoral Shangri-la from the rest of the world and its worries. Usually, the most threatening thing one encounters here is an occasional California highway patrol car.

Mariners see this shoreline differently, however. For them it is fraught with dangers—rocks and reefs waiting to destroy any ship that strays off course.

Like most of this coastline, Point Arena turns a hospitable face to those who come by land but bares its teeth to sailors. Some two and a half miles offshore, predatory Point Arena Rock rises from the sea, waiting to tear open the stoutest hulls. For the unwary, Point Arena Lighthouse flashes out its two-million-candle-power warning: "Don't come too close."

Now fully automated, the light was first lit on May 1, 1870. The original station had two twelve-inch-diameter steam whistles protruding from its fog-signal building. The steam for the whistles was generated by wood-burning boilers that consumed up to one hundred tons of firewood during especially foggy years.

The station's outbuildings included a barn, laundry shed, and hen house, all spotlessly whitewashed, as were the fog-signal building and the lighthouse. Like Point Arena itself, the station had an idyllic outward appearance, but when seen from another angle, it was

The steep, rocky cliffs below the Point Arena Lighthouse show how California's fault lines have scarred and twisted the land. Not surprisingly, the ocean bottom off this coast is littered with sharp, ship-killing rocks.

somewhat less hospitable. Keepers had to share the two-and-a-half-story residence with three assistants, together with all their wives and children. The arrangement afforded little privacy and even less peace and quiet, as noted in an 1880 log entry: "Threatening weather and fighting children."

Keepers complained about the cramped living conditions but were ignored. It took an earthquake to bring improvements. On April 18, 1906, the trembling earth leveled much of San Francisco and devastated the Point Arena Lighthouse. While the station was being rebuilt, the keepers and their families had to live in tents. But much to their relief, the repair effort included construction of four new, freestanding residences.

The new light tower saw improvements as well. It was raised to a height of 115 feet—the original tower had been 100 feet tall. Builders employed reinforced concrete, a revolutionary technique in lighthouse construction, but one that would become standard.

Because of the threat of earthquakes, the Point Arena tower was secured by massive concrete buttresses at its base. This gave the tower the appearance of an obelisk standing on a pedestal but also made it very strong. It has survived numerous earth tremors and even a brush with a navy dirigible.

HOW TO GET THERE: *To reach the Point Area Lighthouse, take Lighthouse Road north from the town of Point Arena. The local Lighthouse Keepers Association offers tours of the lighthouse and fog-signal buildings. The lighthouse is open 11:00 A.M. to 2:30 P.M. daily. For more information call (877) 725–4448 or write P.O. Box 11, Point Arena, CA 95468.*

Perfectly framed by a window in the fog-signal building, the reinforced-concrete Point Arena tower rises 115 feet into the California sky.

POINT REYES LIGHT

Point Reyes National Seashore – 1870

ighthouse keepers never considered Point Reyes among the most desirable duty stations, and it is not hard to see why. The winds howl constantly, there are frequent driving rains, and the point is socked in by an incredible 2,700 hours of fog a year. Added to the discomforts of wind and weather were the 638 steps that had to be climbed to reach the tower and foghorn house from the keeper's dwelling.

Perhaps after a particularly taxing climb in the

The Point Reyes tower as it appeared during the late nineteenth century. (Courtesy U.S. Coast Guard)

teeth of yet another ferocious gale, keeper E. G. Chamberlain quoted the following poetic lines in 1885: "Solitude, where are the charms that sages have seen in thy face? Better dwell in the midst of alarms then reign in this horrible place."

With the coming of electricity, modern communications systems, and improved transportation, the lot of Point Reyes keepers improved. But the horrible weather and winds, sometimes clocked in excess of 100 miles per hour, at the very least kept them acquainted with their former miseries. The station was finally automated in 1975, much to the relief, no doubt, of some wind-battered keeper. Today the property is maintained by the National Park Service as a historic site.

Although it reaches an elevation of more than 600 feet at one location, most of Point Reyes is relatively low. A narrow finger of land, it curves seaward for ten miles. From the sea its highest point often appears to be an island rising abruptly from the water. This illusion has lured more than one vessel to destruction.

In 1595 the Spanish ship *San Agustin,* bound from the Philippines to Acapulco, Mexico, with 130 tons of cargo and a crew of seventy, sought shelter here from a storm. Instead of safe harbor the ship found dangerous shallows and ran aground in Drake's Bay. The vessel's Portuguese master, Captain Sebastian Rodriguez Cermeño, had to skirmish with the local Indians to salvage what he could from the ruined ship. In spite of his best efforts, most of the cargo and food supplies were lost, along with twelve of his men.

Despite the *San Agustin* wreck and many other disasters that followed, Point Reyes remained unmarked for more than 275 years. Congress authorized construction of a lighthouse on Point Reyes in 1852, but government officials spent seventeen years wrangling with local owners over the price of land. Not until 1869 was the Lighthouse Board able to purchase a site—eighty-three acres for $6,000. The price included rights to firewood and water as well as access to a nearby granite quarry.

By the late fall of 1870, a forty-foot-high, sixteen-

Frequently torn by high winds, rugged Point Reyes is one of the foggiest places in America. The light here has been warning ships since 1870.

sided tower encased in iron plate stood on the point, some 294 feet above the sea. The two-ton, first-order Fresnel lens was put in place, and on the night of December 1 the lamp was lit.

HOW TO GET THERE: *The Point Reyes Lighthouse is located at Point Reyes National Seashore, at the end of Sir Francis Drake Highway off California Route 1 northwest of San Francisco. This wild seashore is home to fox, elk, and even mountain lions. There is also an Indian village, and the point is a good spot to watch for migrating gray whales. The squat lighthouse clings to a narrow rocky point. Access to more than 300 steps leading down to the lighthouse is prohibited when winds exceed 40 mph. Views are frequently obscured by fog. Point Reyes is, in fact, one of the foggiest places in the United States. Visitors should begin at the Bear Valley visitors center, near the seashore entrance. The visitors center and lighthouse are open 10:00 A.M. to 4:30 P.M. Thursday through Monday, year-round, and are closed on Tuesday and Wednesday. For information call (415) 669–1534.*

One of America's most beautiful lighthouses commands Point Bonita, which is constantly at war with the sea. As the weathered arch of volcanic rock above clearly shows, someday the sea will win. The narrow wooden suspension bridge was built in 1954 after a massive landslide severed the station's access to the mainland.

CHAPTER TWO

LIGHTS OF THE GOLDEN GATE

San Francisco Bay

he urgent need for lighthouses along the nation's newly acquired and dangerous West Coast first became apparent during the gold rush. Ships crammed with fervently hopeful prospectors and other would-be millionaires arrived in California daily during and after the height of the big rush in 1849. Most of these ships deposited their human cargo at San Francisco, but to get there they first had to pass by the rocky Farallon Islands, which rose out of the open Pacific about twenty-three miles from California's famed Golden Gate. The islands served as a signpost pointing the way to San Francisco Bay, but they were also a deadly hazard. Many fine vessels and brave seamen met their end on the sharp Farallon rocks. So when Congress selected locations for the West Coast's first lighthouses during the early 1850s, the Farallons stood near the top of the list.

Ironically, a group of rowdy gold-rush freebooters, nearly all of whom had reached California by sea, did their best to scuttle plans for a lighthouse in the Farallons. It seemed these particular forty-niners were more interested in eggs than in gold, and they saw the U.S. government and its Lighthouse Service as claim jumpers.

THE GREAT FARALLON EGG WAR

In San Francisco chicken eggs were as scarce as hens' teeth and were selling for upwards of a dollar each. These extraordinary prices touched off a new sort of rush as bands of armed men set sail for the Farallons, where seabirds nested in vast rookeries. There they robbed the nests of hapless murres and gulls and took the eggs back to the city, where they cashed them in for considerable sums. Many of these "egg miners" were unsuccessful prospectors. Having found no gold in their pans, they resolved to provide some gold—at a respectable profit—for the frying pans of their fellow gold diggers.

Then came the U.S. Lighthouse Service with plans for a light station on Southeast Farallon, the largest of the islands. The nest robbers were convinced that a flashing navigational light and fog signal here would drive away the seabirds and ruin their burgeoning egg business. The jagged rocks of the seven-mile-long island chain threatened destruction and death to increasing numbers of ships, crews, and passengers headed for the Golden Gate, but this was of little concern to the egg gatherers. They were businessmen, and this was the West—the land of opportunity.

The forty-niner egg men were not the first to exploit the island wildlife. The name *Farallons* is derived from the description given the islands in the logbooks of early Spanish explorers, who called them *los Farallons,* meaning the "small, pointed islands." No doubt the Spanish, too, gathered eggs from the abundant nests of seabirds. In 1579 the buccaneer and globe-circling explorer Sir Francis Drake reputedly stopped here so his crew could gather eggs and harpoon seals to restock his ship's empty larder. Beginning in 1810 Russian sealing expeditions from Alaska set up camp in the Farallons. By the end of their third hunting season in the islands, they had taken 200,000 seal pelts. In 1819 and 1820 Americans hunted sea lions here and salted the meat to feed U.S. soldiers in the Oregon Territory. But none of this activity compared with

A fanciful view of the South Farallon Island Light Station. The drawing was made during the 1850s at a time when San Francisco poachers warred over the rich harvest of eggs they stole from island seabirds. (Courtesy National Archives)

This aerial view of the South Farallon Island Light depicts the station as it looked in 1925.
(Courtesy National Archives)

the intense rapaciousness of the gold-rush egg gatherers. In a single boatload they carried off 12,000 eggs to San Francisco.

So lucrative was the egg business that various groups of poachers fell into fierce competition. Brawls and gunfights broke out when rival gangs encountered one another amid the rocks, nests, and bird droppings of the Farallons. Their battles grew so frequent and so intense that collectively they became known as the Farallon Island Egg War. The combatants even wore uniforms—baggy shirts fitted with huge pockets for gathering eggs.

In 1852 the bark *Oriole* arrived off Southeast Farallon, the largest of the islets, with a construction crew and a load of materials for building lighthouses. The vessel and the workers were turned back by an angry mob of gun-toting egg-shirted poachers.

At this the Lighthouse Service decided to get tough and dispatched a steamer, loaded not just with construction materials but with a detachment of well-armed troops. When the egg pickers saw this impressive show of force, they backed down, and construction of the light station commenced. But hostile pickers, whose activities were eventually consolidated under the umbrella of the Farallon Egg Company, continued to make a nuisance of themselves for at least twenty-five years.

Even as the pickers continued to rob nests, workmen began the exhausting task of quarrying rock from the island to form the shell of a forty-one-foot tower. Stone and bricks were lugged to the construction site near the 317-foot summit of a hill on Southeast Farallon. A dwelling for the keeper was built on a level area nearer the sea. By 1853 everything was in place but the light.

One year later a French freighter arrived in San Francisco with a most welcome cargo—a large shipment of wine and a sparkling new first-order Fresnel lens for the Farallon Lighthouse. As it turned out, however, the enormous, eight-foot-diameter lens proved much too big for the light tower and its lantern room. The construction contractors, partners Kelly and Gibbons from Baltimore, were forced to tear down the tower and rebuild it from the ground up. As a consequence of the delay, the light was not in place and ready to be lit until January 1, 1856, more than three years after the project was launched.

Two years later a much-needed fog signal was added. The signal was of a revolutionary design: It was powered by air forced through a blowhole by natural wave action. Like many clever innovations, this one had an unexpected and critical flaw. On the California coast fog is usually accompanied by flat calms. As a result, when the fog signal was most needed, it barely functioned, if at all. Despite its questionable usefulness, the blowhole foghorn remained in operation until storm waves smashed the contraption in 1871 and it was replaced by a more conventional steam-powered fog signal.

THE SECOND EGG WAR

The fears of the egg pickers proved unjustified. The murres and gulls ignored the blat of the foghorn, the flashing light, and even the quarrelsome poachers who continually robbed their nests. Vast flocks continued to nest on the remote Farallons.

Some of the light station's early keepers joined in the poaching to earn a little extra "egg" money. They also hunted seals, whose powdered whiskers were sold in San Francisco's Chinatown as an aphrodisiac.

In 1881 the egg wars, quieted by the formation of the Farallon Egg Company, flared up once again. A rival group of egg pickers deeply resented the company's domination of the Farallon nests and resolved to break its monopoly. The dispute came to a head when several boatloads of armed men landed on the islands and a pitched battle ensued. The gunfire brought a din of protests from thousands of squawking seabirds. It also brought to the islands a U.S. marshal and a platoon of soldiers, who promptly evicted the trigger-happy egg pickers and burned their huts.

Nonetheless, egg picking on the Farallons continued well into the 1890s. The Lighthouse Service reached the end of its patience when an assistant keeper fell and broke both of his legs while helping the pickers gather eggs. Soon afterward the service decreed that no one be allowed to land on the islands without prior written approval from the District Superintendent of Lighthouses in San Francisco. Still the poachers came, despite occasional confrontations with keepers and police. Finally, it was not lawmen but the prodigious egg-laying capacity of California chickens that put an end to the poaching. People started eating chicken eggs by the dozen, and the market for the seabird variety dwindled to nothing.

The Farallons became a bird sanctuary in 1909. Today the islands are visited mostly by naturalists and bird fanciers who probably don't eat gulls' eggs for breakfast.

Keepers and their families lived in comfortable isolation at East Brother Lighthouse from 1874 until it was handed over to local preservationists during the 1970s. Today this still-functioning lighthouse offers travelers a unique bed-and-breakfast experience as well as a glimpse at the life of lighthouse keepers.

THE LONELINESS OF ISLAND KEEPERS

The disappearance of the egg pickers left only the birds, seals, lighthouse keepers, and their families on the islands. The loneliness of this remote light station, more than twenty miles from land, soon became legendary. For many years supply boats called on the island only four times annually.

Sometimes the families of keepers suffered because of their isolation. The government had trouble hiring teachers for the keepers' children. The stir-crazy teachers usually resigned and left the islands within a few months. Tragically, at least three sick children died on Southeast Farallon because their parents could not get them to the mainland in time to receive proper medical attention.

Gradually, life at the Farallon Lighthouse improved. During World War I the navy placed a communication station on the Farallons, and navy tugs made frequent visits. Radios brought music and dance parties, and the keepers even built a tennis court. When the last keeper was removed at the time the station was automated in 1972, he was probably very sorry to go. After all, isolation can be splendid.

The Farallon Islands lie very near the imaginary line that, in the minds of most, divides northern and southern California. Because of the role they played in the great California gold rush, these islands serve as an appropriate entryway to the "Golden Gate."

POINT BONITA LIGHT

San Francisco – 1855 AND 1877

Mariners approaching San Francisco from the west often scan the horizon, looking for the bright beacon of Point Bonita Lighthouse. They know it points the way to the Golden Gate, the bay, and the city's bustling harbor. They also see it as a warning to keep well away from Point Bonita itself and its deadly rocks.

The federal West Coast Survey, completed in 1850, recognized the importance of Point Bonita and recommended that a light be placed there. Nothing was done, however, until a series of wrecks on or near the point forced the govern-

Perched precariously above the Pacific, Point Bonita Lighthouse marks the seaward approach to the Golden Gate. The suspension bridge links the station to the mainland. (Courtesy U.S. Coast Guard)

ment to act. Steaming through a dense early-morning fog on New Year's Day in 1851, the 1,275-ton side-wheeler *Tennessee* struck rocks near the point and was lost. Underwriters estimated the value of the unsalvageable ship and cargo to be $300,000, a very large sum at the time. Three years later, the Pacific clipper ship *San Francisco* slammed into the point and sank.

Faced with these and other wrecks on or near Point Bonita, officials moved ahead with plans to place a lighthouse and fog signal there. Built in 1855 on a high ledge more than 300 feet above the sea, the original station had a fifty-six-foot brick tower and a detached, Cape Cod–style dwelling. Officials considered this lighthouse so important that they assigned it an exceptionally powerful second-order Fresnel lens. The light could be seen from up to twenty miles at sea, except in a heavy fog, which could make it completely invisible.

The station's fog signal consisted of a surplus army cannon fired off with an earsplitting roar by the keepers whenever fog rolled in, which it did nearly every day. The cannon was eventually replaced by a 1,500-pound bell, which keepers struck with a hammer to warn fog-bound sailors away from the point. The light itself did not always offer much warning in a fog. Because it stood so far up on the cliff, its beacon was frequently masked by fog or low-hanging clouds. To solve this problem, officials decided in 1872 to build another lighthouse closer to the water.

Construction of the new tower on a frightfully narrow ledge about 120 feet above the waves was no simple matter. To bring materials to the site, a landing platform, derrick, and incline railway had to be built and a tunnel blasted through more than one hundred feet of solid rock. The new station, consisting of a thirty-three-foot tower, a fog-signal building with a pair of steam-driven sirens, and storage buildings, took more than five years to complete. Fitted with the Fresnel lens from the original lighthouse, the station was, at last, ready for service.

Keeper John B. Brown lit the lamps of the new Point Bonita Lighthouse for the first time on the evening of February 1, 1877. Brown served at the point for more than twenty years, retiring just before the turn of the century. It is said that during his long term of service, Brown pulled more than forty shipwrecked sailors out of the pounding surf below the lighthouse.

Although precariously perched on an exposed rock, the Point Bonita tower survived the great San Francisco earthquake, which struck at 5:12 A.M. on April 12, 1906. While most other station buildings remained intact, the keeper's dwelling, which had stood for more than half a century, was shaken to its foundations. Fortunately, the keeper and his family managed to run out of the house before it collapsed, and no one at the station was injured. Like many other quake-stricken residents of the San Francisco area, the keeper's family had to take refuge in makeshift accommodations—in this case the oil-storage building—until a new residence could be built.

During the 1940s a landslide destroyed the land bridge that connected the tower and fog-signal building. The Coast Guard first replaced it with a wooden bridge, then with the scenic suspension bridge that still serves the station today.

In 1981 the Point Bonita Light became the last of California's lighthouses to be automated. Today, it is part of the Golden Gate National Recreation Area.

HOW TO GET THERE: *This extraordinarily scenic lighthouse is located off Highway 101, just north of San Francisco. To reach it from the city, cross the Golden Gate Bridge and take the first exit (Alexander Avenue). Then take Conzelman Road and follow signs to the lighthouse. The winding road to Point Bonita provides spectacular views of the city and coast. You should bring sensible shoes, since reaching the lighthouse requires a hike of more than a mile. Contact the Golden Gate National Recreation Area, Fort Mason, Building 201, San Francisco, CA 94123; (415) 556–0560.*

ike a giant wedding cake set atop a pedestal, the original Mile Rocks Lighthouse consisted of a series of cylinders stacked one atop the other. This extraordinary building was demolished in 1966. (Courtesy Herman Jaehne)

FORT POINT LIGHT

San Francisco – 1855 AND 1864

Completed in 1853, at about the same time as the original Alcatraz Island Lighthouse, the Fort Point Lighthouse stood empty for more than a year, waiting for its third-order Fresnel lens to arrive from France. This light had an important job to do—that of marking the channel through the Golden Gate and into San Francisco Bay—but the powerful lens was never installed, and the tower's lamps were never lit. Before the station could be placed in operation, the lighthouse was torn down to make way for the massive brick walls of Fort Winfield Scott. The Fresnel lens originally intended for Fort Point was given instead to Point Pinos Lighthouse on Monterey Bay, where it continues to serve after more than 145 years.

While the three-story fortress was under construction, workers built a wooden light tower outside its walls. Employing a fifth-order lens, it served until 1864, when storm-driven Pacific waves blasted through a seawall and threatened to undermine the foundations of the fort. To make way for a larger, more stable seawall, the Fort Point Lighthouse had to be torn down for a second time. It was replaced by a twenty-seven-foot iron skeleton-tower perched atop the walls of the fort itself. The additional height made the light easier for approaching sailors to spot.

The station served its purpose faithfully for more than seven decades, until construction of the Golden Gate Bridge made the old lighthouse obsolete, and it was discontinued in 1934. Towering 740 feet above the sea, the bridge itself is a mammoth lighthouse. Mariners can see its lights and recognize the distinctive inverted arches of its supporting cables from many miles at sea. Completed in 1937, the bridge is one of the world's most recognizable land and sea marks.

During its active years the Fort Point Light station played a role in one of the worst maritime disasters in San Francisco Bay history. In 1901 the Pacific Mail Steamship Company's passenger freighter *City of Rio de Janeiro* was about to complete a Pacific crossing from Hong Kong. Pushing into the bay's brackish waters in a thick fog, the *Rio*'s Captain William Ward lost the main channel and, unable to hear the fog bell at Fort Point, slammed into a ledge of rock. The *Rio* sank quickly, with a loss of 140 lives. Captain Ward went down with his ship.

HOW TO GET THERE: *The old lighthouse can still be seen standing atop the walls of Fort Winfield Scott, now part of the Fort Point National Historical Site. To reach the fort, follow Lincoln Boulevard toward the Golden Gate and turn left onto Long Avenue. The site is open every day from 10:00 A.M. to 5:00 P.M., except on major holidays. For more information call (415) 556–1693.*

(Courtesy John W. Weil)

The metal Fort Point tower stands on top of the massive, brick walls of Fort Winfield Scott, which once protected San Francisco Bay from enemy warships. The fort and lighthouse are now part of a national historical park. (Courtesy John W. Weil)

ALCATRAZ ISLAND LIGHT

San Francisco – 1854 AND 1909

At night, from almost any point along the San Francisco waterfront or in the hills above, one can see the bright flash of a lighthouse beacon calling from an island well out in the bay. Even to visitors and tourists it is a comforting and familiar sight, for, like the nearby Golden Gate Bridge, the lighthouse in the bay is among the images we invariably associate with this remarkable city.

As almost any schoolchild knows, the rocky island on which the lighthouse stands is Alcatraz, a name indelibly stamped on the American psyche. To this day, the name has a forbidding ring to it, suggesting an isolated and sinister place, and no wonder. For more than thirty years, Alcatraz Island was the site of a maximum-security federal penitentiary where some of the nation's most notorious criminals were incarcerated—Al Capone was an unwilling guest there during the 1930s. The Alcatraz "Pen" had a well-earned reputation as a "hard-time" prison, and the cold, shark-infested waters surrounding the island made it almost escape-proof. Perhaps understandably, prisoners came to hate the name "Alcatraz" so much that they could barely speak it, referring to their unhappy home only as "the Rock."

Ironically, the word *alcatraz* is innocuous enough—it is Spanish for *pelican.* The name is fitting, since the island has always been very popular among big birds with shovel beaks. It has never been well liked by mariners, however. Standing astride one of the busiest shipping channels on earth, the island is a formidable threat to pilots and their vessels, especially when the bay is blanketed in fog, as is so often the case. For this reason, among others, officials selected Alcatraz as the site for one of the first U.S. lighthouses in the West.

During the heady gold-rush years of the mid-1800s, San Francisco was a robust frontier port through which funneled countless thousands of doggedly optimistic prospectors on their way to the gold fields in the Sierra foothills. Only a tiny percentage of California's "forty-niners" turned their golden dreams into real, bankable riches. Luckily, for those who did not strike it rich, the West had far more to offer than gold. There was such an abundance of land and resources here that anyone with a little horse sense and a willingness to work hard could at least make himself *feel* rich.

Suggesting a ruined medieval fortress, the Alcatraz penitentiary is now abandoned, but the island's lighthouse remains active. (Courtesy U.S. Coast Guard)

Seen in ruins on the right, the Alcatraz Lighthouse keeper's residence burned during the island's occupation by Native American protesters in 1969. (Courtesy Bob and Sandra Shanklin)

Very early on, people began to see the San Francisco Bay as the doorway to the West. Through the Golden Gate, with its Gibraltarlike ramparts, would flow the settlers and materials needed to populate and build up a new and prosperous region. Recognizing this, Congress appropriated funds to build one lighthouse after another to guide ships into San Francisco's harbor or up the Sacramento River. Begun in 1852, the Alcatraz Lighthouse was completed the following year, but it was not placed in service until June 1854, shortly after its third-order Fresnel lens arrived by ship from France. This, nonetheless, made it the first operational U.S. lighthouse in the West.

A one-and-a-half-story Cape Cod–style dwelling with a short tower peeking just above its roof, the Alcatraz Island Lighthouse served well for more than sixty years. Then, like most other structures in and around San Francisco, it suffered serious damage in the earthquake of 1906. Instead of repairing the badly shaken building, officials decided to build a new lighthouse. This one was given a spacious bay-style dwelling and an octagonal tower of reinforced concrete. The new tower was eighty-four feet tall, more than enough to lift the light above the high walls of a recently constructed military prison. Standing on the island's high-est point, the octagonal tower placed the light more than 200 feet above the waters of the bay.

The Alcatraz Island keepers never felt entirely comfortable living and working in such close proximity to a prison. Their neighborhood deteriorated even further when the old military prison was made a federal penitentiary in 1934. Sometimes events at the prison placed the keepers' lives in danger, as happened during a deadly two-day riot in 1946. U.S. Marines were brought in to quell the uprising, but while many inmates and guards were killed, none of the keepers were injured. Ironically, the station was automated in 1963, about the time the penitentiary was closed.

Another violent chapter in the Alcatraz story came in 1969, when militant Native Americans took over the island and held it for more than a year. During the occupation, the lovely old keeper's dwelling was burned.

HOW TO GET THERE: *Alcatraz Island and its lighthouse are part of the Golden Gate National Recreation Area; call (415) 705–1042. Regular tours of the island, prison, and lighthouse facilities are offered at Pier 41 in the Fisherman's Wharf area. For information and reservations call (415) 705–5555 or (415) 773–1188.*

YERBA BUENA LIGHT

San Francisco – 1874

oday, a Coast Guard admiral lives in the Victorian-style keeper's dwelling of the old Yerba Buena Lighthouse, built in 1874. Not surprisingly, the admiral does not actually tend the light—automated since 1958—but he is a lighthouse keeper of sorts. Under his command are the Coast Guard personnel who keep the navigational lights of the California coast and San Francisco Bay burning.

The 140-acre island serves as a Coast Guard station, depot, and communications center from which San Francisco Bay lights and fog signals are still monitored. Years ago, lighthouse supply ships and tenders, such as the side-wheeler *Shubrick* and the steamer *Manzanita,* were berthed here. Lightships such as the *San Francisco* were sometimes brought to the depot for refitting and maintenance. The island also served as a center of operations for buoy placement and maintenance.

The Yerba Buena Lighthouse was intended primarily to serve passenger boats and ferries passing back and forth between the San Francisco and Oakland sides of the bay. Ferry traffic was greatly reduced after the opening of the San Francisco–Oakland Bay Bridge in 1939, but the lighthouse remained in service to guard the island and guide shipping down the bay. The original fourth-order Fresnel lens still shines from the station's two-story octagonal tower, displaying a fixed, white light. The lens is even older than the Yerba Buena station, having first served at Oregon's Yaquina Bay Lighthouse.

Years before the Lighthouse Service built its depot on Yerba Buena, Costanoan Indians would come to the island by canoe to gather reeds and herd goats. After the U.S. Army established a camp here in 1873, the Indians no longer visited the island, but their goats remained. For many years the hardy animals roamed free over the island, occasionally chewing up insulation, damaging stored materials, and generally making a nuisance of themselves.

In 1836 the far-ranging trading brig *Alert* sailed into San Francisco Bay and anchored near Yerba Buena Island. Among the able-bodied seamen aboard the *Alert* was Richard Henry Dana, who would later include descriptions of the island, the bay, and the San Francisco Peninsula in his *Two Years Before the Mast.* Dana believed the bay would one day become the center of western commercial development.

HOW TO GET THERE: *Yerba Buena Lighthouse is located on an active Coast Guard station and is off limits to the public. Its light can be seen from boats in the bay and from a variety of points along the shore.*

The upper building of the Yerba Buena Island Lighthouse is the former keeper's dwelling.

(Courtesy U.S. Coast Guard)

BLUNTS REEF LIGHTSHIP (WAL–605)
Oakland – 1950

There are many navigational obstacles and channels that are impossible to mark with a lighthouse. In the past, when lights were needed over deep open water, as at Blunts Reef near Eureka, California, or San Francisco Station outside the Golden Gate, the Coast Guard assigned lightships to the task. These small vessels rode at anchor in all conditions, often for many months at a time, holding lights aloft on one or more high masts. Usually, they had onboard fog signals ready to blast warnings to approaching ships whenever visibility was impaired by the weather.

One such vessel was the Lightship *WAL–605*, which served for nearly ten years at Blunts Reef off Eureka. Launched in 1950 at a shipyard in East Boothbay, Maine, the *WAL–605* was originally assigned to Overfalls Station near Cape May, New Jersey. In 1960 it was sent to the West for service at Blunts Reef. During its last years on active duty with the Coast Guard—it was retired in 1975—the *WAL–605* served as a relief lightship at San Francisco Station or wherever it was needed.

Sold as surplus property by the Coast Guard, the *WAL–605* later functioned as a historical museum and even as a fishing boat. Today it is owned by the nonprofit Lighthouse Society in Oakland, which is doing lighthouse lovers, students of maritime history, and the nation an enormous favor by restoring the old ship.

The *WAL–605* has a steel hull 108 feet long with a 30-foot beam. The mushroom-shaped anchor, which so often held it firmly on station, weighs 7,000 pounds. Currently under restoration, the lightship is berthed on the Oakland waterfront.

HOW TO GET THERE: *When restoration is complete, the Lighthouse Society plans to move the lightship to a permanent berth in the San Francisco Bay area. For information concerning its status and location, call the society at (415) 362–7255. The society can also provide a wealth of facts and information on lighthouses and lightships throughout the United States and Canada and on general lighthouse history. You may want to join. Write to United States Lighthouse Society, 244 Kearney Street, 5th Floor, San Francisco, CA 94108.*

The Blunts Reef Lightship WAL-605 *on station in the Pacific. Lightships often rode at anchor for months at a time warning ships away from hazards such as deadly Blunts Reef near Eureka, California. Today,* WAL-605 *is being restored for use as a floating museum in Oakland.* (Courtesy U.S. Coast Guard)

EAST BROTHER LIGHT

Richmond – **1874**

uilt in 1874, the classically Victorian East Brother Lighthouse serves a pair of functions nowadays. While its light still shines, guiding vessels into San Pablo Bay and the Sacramento/San Joaquin River estuaries, it is also a popular bed-and-breakfast inn. One could hardly imagine a more appealing place to spend the weekend. Listed on the National Register of Historic Places, the old lighthouse is located on an island just off San Pablo Point. From their rooms or the gallery at the top of the tower, guests can gaze out across the water to San Francisco and the coastal mountains of the Marin Peninsula. Sunsets here are spectacular.

As early as the 1860s, maritime officials saw the need for a lighthouse and fog signal to mark the channel through the narrow and often treacherous San Pablo Straits. Unable to buy property on the mainland at an acceptable price, the government resorted to building the station on tiny East Brother Island. Construction crews had to blast away much of the one-third-acre island in order to level the site. There was hardly room on what remained to squeeze the combi-nation two-story tower and dwelling and separate fog-signal building.

Although the isolated station was extremely confining, keepers often lived here with their families, and several gen-erations of children were born on the island. When children reached school age, teachers rowed out from the mainland to give them lessons. Mail and supplies had to be brought by rowboat from San Quentin, a two-mile trip across the bay.

In 1967 the Coast Guard decided to automate the sta-tion, place its light on a pole, and tear down the old build-ings. Tireless protests on the part of the conservationists and local residents saved the structures. Repaired and remodeled again and again over the years, the tower and residence had lost much of their original Victorian charm. Using grants and donations, a citizen's group restored them to their orig-inal glory. The light is still in operation.

HOW TO GET THERE: *For reservations, direc-tions, or information about transportation to East Brother Island, call (510) 233–2385.*

A gargantuan container ship safely navigates past Pigeon Point, thanks in part to the 130-year-old lighthouse that stands guard here. Years before the station's 115-foot tower was built in 1872, a clipper ship called the Carrier Pigeon *wrecked here and gave the point its name.*

CHAPTER THREE

LIGHTS OF THE BIG SUR
Central California

For travelers who love beautiful scenery, the central coast of California is an earthly paradise. Here a bold range of geologically young mountains meets the planet's oldest and most extensive ocean. Here fluffy blankets of morning fog lay siege to craggy desert peaks. When the fog lifts, it reveals a wonderland of infinite ocean vistas, wave-swept rocks, cliffs that drop dizzyingly into the sea, and lush ravines that nurture hidden groves of ancient redwoods. And all of it is painted in a swirl of van Gogh colors.

Whether seen from land or water, this coast is enchanting, but mariners know it is not just for its beauty. To them it is a place of danger. Colonial-era Spanish treasure ships, bearing gold and spices from the Orient, crossed 5,000 miles of the open Pacific to reach California, but during many weeks at sea, they were seldom so threatened as when they approached these shores. Often, the coastline was draped in fog and all but invisible. A captain's first warning of a landfall might be the grinding and splintering of his hull on stone. Or a storm might blow up suddenly and send his ship hurtling out of control toward the rocks and certain destruction. Many of these ships and their crews simply vanished, never to be seen or heard from again. No one knows how many Spanish wrecks may lie in the waters off California. No doubt, there are more than a few.

The carnage off this coast extends right up to our own times. Even with coastal lights, the best charts, and the finest navigational instruments to guide them, sailors still get lost here. And sometimes the results are disastrous.

A FLEET OF DESTROYERS GOES DOWN

On the evening of September 8, 1923, an impressive flotilla of fourteen U.S. Navy destroyers pushed south from San Francisco on its way to San Diego. Under the overall command of Captain Edward Watson, the destroyers maintained a precise military formation, running one behind the other about two minutes apart. Despite a thick fog cloaking both the sea and the shoreline just to the east, the flotilla was making good time, steaming steadily ahead at twenty knots.

In order to maintain a uniform distance from the shore, Captain Watson intended to turn his flotilla to the east once the destroyers had passed Point Conception, where the California coastline itself changes course. This critical shift in the direction of the shoreline is marked by a pair of lights, one on Point Arguello and a more powerful one on Point Conception. Peering into the darkness, Captain Watson had seen neither of the two beacons. Growing impatient, he became increasingly convinced that he had missed the lights in the heavy fog and that the flotilla was now well to the south of Point Conception.

Just as he was about to give the order that would turn his destroyers to the east, supposedly into the Santa Barbara Channel, Watson received a surprising message from the *Delphy,* the lead vessel in the flotilla. The *Delphy's* navigator reported receiving the signal of the radio beacon on Point Arguello. The flotilla commander was momentarily puzzled. If the report was accurate and the signal was the one from Point Arguello, then the *Delphy* and the rest of the flotilla were still well to the north of Point Conception. The captain decided his navigator must be mistaken. For one thing, the flotilla was receiving a second radio signal that seemed to indicate the destroyers had cleared Conception. For another, Captain Watson was an old sailor who trusted his instinct for dead reckoning more than any navigational contraption. He gave the order.

Unfortunately for the flotilla commander and his destroyers, the second signal had been false and the captain's reckoning was mistaken. Shortly after the vessels began their turn to the east, chaos broke at a place called Honda, a mile or so north of Point Arguello Lighthouse. Metal screamed and ruptured boilers hissed as the Delphy and, one after another, the *Lee, Young, Woodbury, Chauncey, Nicholas,* and *Fuller* slammed into the shore, striking the rocks at approximately two-minute intervals.

Lighthouse keepers Gotford Olson, Arvel Settles, and Jesse Mygrants could hear the drumming of engines as the destroyers steamed at near top speed toward their doom. For the keepers it was a hellish night filled with the grinding of metal against stone and desperate cries for help. Olson, Settles, and Mygrants pulled many of the shipwrecked sailors out of the surf. Injured men were bandaged and treated at the lighthouse. Later the keepers would receive commendations from the navy for their efforts.

In all, seven of the ships went aground that night. Another seven managed to turn away in time and run for open water and safety. Twenty-three sailors lost their lives and many others were injured. In memory of the ships and men lost in this tragic mishap, a memorial anchor was placed at Honda on a bluff overlooking the site of the wrecks.

THE LAST HOURS OF A MIGHTY AIRSHIP

At about 5:00 P.M. on February 12, 1935, awestruck keeper Thomas Henderson saw a huge dark shape filling the sky to the west of the Point Sur Lighthouse. This was no fog bank or squall line likely to rush in off the Pacific and batter the point. Instead, it was an enormous naval vessel—only this ship floated, not on the water, but in the air.

She was the USS *Macon*, one of the biggest U.S. Navy ships that ever flew. A rigid airship much like those made famous by the German Zeppelin company, the *Macon* was designed by German engineers and built in America. Intended for use as a naval scout ship, she kept several airplanes in an onboard hangar and could launch and retrieve them during flight.

The *Macon* was one of three experimental airships built for the navy. The others were the USS *Shenandoah*, downed by an Ohio thunderstorm in 1925, and the USS *Akron*, a nearly identical sister ship of the *Macon*. The *Akron* went down in an Atlantic gale in 1933 with a loss of seventy-three lives. Launched just three weeks after the destruction of the *Akron*, the *Macon* 's fate would be much like that of her predecessors.

During her maiden voyage in 1933, the *Macon* attracted a swarm of media attention wherever she went. Some of this publicity she generated herself—for instance, by dropping mail and postcards to President Franklin Delano Roosevelt while he was on vacation in the Pacific. But much of the public's fascination with the airship was due to her extraordinary size. When she flew over a town, she would literally blot out the sun. More than 780 feet long and 130 feet in diameter at her widest point, she could have accommodated several jet airliners inside her if she were still around today. In fact, the *Macon* was longer than three Boeing 747 jumbo jets parked end to end.

Her frame was made of a lightweight but super-strong aluminum alloy. Arranged in a series of huge rings that gave the ship its characteristic zeppelin shape, the frame was covered in a skin of cotton cloth painted with a reflective airplane dope. She weighed 240,000 pounds and was filled

A romantic view of Point Sur Lighthouse. *The dirigible* Macon *crashed near here in 1935.*

The original Santa Cruz Lighthouse was razed in 1948, but was eventually replaced by this lovely replica, built as a memorial to a young surfer killed near this spot. (Courtesy Bob and Sandra Shanklin)

with helium, stored in twelve separate cells. The helium could lift her safely only about a mile, so the *Macon*'s operational ceiling was below 5,000 feet. For this reason, she was most effective when launched from sea level. Obviously, the big ship would not have been used much in Colorado.

Keeper Henderson was as impressed with the *Macon* as anyone, but ironically, he would be among the last to see her. When Henderson spotted the zeppelin, she was fighting a coastal squall. Only moments after he focused his binoculars on her, one of the *Macon*'s tail fins broke loose from her stern structural ring. Apparently, this punctured two or more of the helium cells in the stern and set off a chain of events that doomed the big ship. With the loss of buoyancy, the crew dropped masses of water ballast in order to keep the dirigible aloft. This sent the now out-of-control *Macon* racing skyward to very near her maximum safe altitude of 5,000 feet. The rapid ascent threw open a set of safety valves, venting even more precious helium from the ship's remaining cells. Soon the *Macon* no longer had enough helium to keep her aloft, and she plunged into the sea. Shortly before 5:40 P.M., the *Macon* struck the water a few miles southwest of Point Sur and immediately began to sink. Within little more than half an hour, she was gone.

From his lofty lighthouse perch at Point Sur, Henderson witnessed the entire *Macon* tragedy, but there was nothing he could do to help. Several naval vessels that happened to be in the area raced to the scene. Almost miraculously, they were able to rescue all but two of the *Macon*'s crew of eighty-three.

POINT MONTARA LIGHT

Pacifica – 1872 AND 1928

In 1868 the steamer *Colorado* ran aground on a ledge within sight of Point Montara. Four years later the freighter *Acuelo* wrecked just below the point, spilling into the sea a cargo of coal and iron worth at least $150,000. The latter disaster led to the placement of a fog signal on Point Montara in 1872. Nearly three decades would pass before a light was added and the Point Montara fog-signal station became a full-fledged lighthouse.

Perched atop a thirty-foot conical tower (the exist-ing structure dates to 1928), the Point Montara Light shines from a point seventy feet above the sea. The light can be seen from about fourteen miles away. Ironically, the original fog-signal building has been removed.

HOW TO GET THERE: *Most of the buildings at the station, including the Victorian keeper's quarters, are now used as a youth hostel. Visitors hours on the grounds are limited: 7:30 to 9:30* A.M. *and 4:30 to 9:30* P.M. *For more information call (415) 728–7177.*

For nearly three decades Point Montara had only a fog signal to warn sailors of its jagged rocks, but in 1900 a lighthouse was added. The light still burns today, but most of the station's buildings are now used as a youth hostel.

PIGEON POINT LIGHT

Pescadero – 1872

ifty miles south of San Francisco, the light at Pigeon Point shines out toward the Pacific from an elevation of nearly 160 feet. Slightly more than forty feet of that height is provided by the point, the rest by the 115-foot brick tower.

The tower, one of the tallest on the Pacific coast, was built in 1872 with brick shipped around Cape Horn from the East. The land, lighthouse, and huge first-order Fresnel lens cost the government approximately $20,000.

Pigeon Point got its name when the Yankee clipper *Carrier Pigeon* wrecked on its rocks in 1853. The 175-foot clipper had been launched in Bath, Maine, the previous year. She was 129 days out of Boston and bound for San Francisco when she ran into a thick fog off the California coast. The ship's captain, Azariah Doane, mistook the point for the Farallon Islands well to the north. The error cost Doane his ship as she ran aground on the point's sharp rocks. Before Doane and his sailors could free her, the *Carrier Pigeon* was pounded to pieces by a gale. What was left of the cargo was sold at the scene of the wreck for a fraction of its original value.

HOW TO GET THERE: *Now open to the public as a hostelry, the Pigeon Point Light station is located south of Pescadero and just north of the Año Nuevo Reserve. The grounds are open all year. A docent leads tours on Sundays from 11:00 A.M. to 3:00 P.M. For information contact Año Nuevo State Reserve, New Years Creek Road, Pescadero, CA 94060; (650) 879–2120.*

The imposing Pigeon Point tower rises 115 feet into the skies above the central California coast. This lighthouse has served mariners since 1872, but nowadays doubles as an attraction at a popular state park.

SANTA CRUZ LIGHT

Santa Cruz, California – **1869 AND 1967**

A lighthouse stood on this site as early as 1869. The brick edifice at the entrance to Santa Cruz Harbor serves as both a harbor marker and a memorial to a young surfer who died near here. The building houses a surfing museum.

HOW TO GET THERE: *The Santa Cruz Lighthouse, rebuilt in 1967, can be reached by driving northwest along West Cliff Drive to Lighthouse Point. The brick structure is now the prime attraction of the Santa Cruz Lighthouse Park and houses a surfing museum. Admission is free. The beaches in this area are excellent for strolling and offer a fine view of the lighthouse. Hours are noon to 4:00 P.M. weekdays except Tuesday, when the museum is closed, and noon to 5:00 P.M. on weekends. Call the Mark Abbot Memorial Lighthouse Museum at (408) 425–7278.*

A replica of the original 1869 Santa Cruz Lighthouse was built on these cliffs in 1967. It serves as both an active aid to navigation and as a surfing museum.

POINT PINOS LIGHT

Pacific Grove – 1855

Now surrounded by a golf course, the West Coast's oldest standing lighthouse is leased by the Coast Guard to a historical society, which uses it as a maritime museum. The forty-three-foot tower rises from the center of the keeper's dwelling, originally granite faced but overlaid with reinforced concrete following a severe shaking by the 1906 San Francisco earthquake. Dormers and a rear roof have been added to the dwelling, but the tower still houses the original light.

Nestled on a southerly point on the Monterey Peninsula at the entrance to Monterey Bay, the Point Pinos Lighthouse has attracted many visitors since it was first lit on February 1, 1855. Among the best-known tourists to enjoy a visit here was Robert Louis Stevenson, author of such classic novels as *Treasure Island* and *Dr. Jekyll and Mr. Hyde*. A popular travel writer as well as a novelist, Stevenson came here in 1871. The keeper, Captain Allen Luce, guided Stevenson around the lighthouse property and even took time out to show the writer his ship models. Stevenson was so charmed by his visit that he included a description of the lighthouse in his travel book *The Old Pacific Coast*.

The first keeper to serve at Point Pinos was an adventurer. An Englishman, Charles Layton had fought honorably for both the British and American armies before he joined in the California gold rush of 1849. But like so many other would-be gold millionaires, Layton found little of value in the goldfields. In 1852 he gave up the search and settled in Monterey with his wife, Charlotte. Within a few years he had won appointment as keeper of the Point Pinos Lighthouse at an annual salary of $1,000 a year—a comfortable sum at the time.

Layton did not live to enjoy his good fortune, however. A few months after he started, he joined a posse chasing the bandito Anastasio García. Layton died from a wound he received in a shootout with García and his men. As often happened when a lighthouse keeper died or became incapacitated, his wife took over his duties. Mrs. Layton faithfully maintained the light and soon was appointed keeper herself.

HOW TO GET THERE: *Located on Lighthouse Avenue between Sunset Drive and Asilomar Avenue in Pacific Grove, the Point Pinos Lighthouse is open to the public only on Saturday and Sunday, 1:00 to 4:00 P.M. For more information call the Pacific Grove Museum at (831) 648–3116. To reach the lighthouse, take California 68 West off Highway 1, then turn left at Asilomar. Sea otters often play in the surf in this area. Nearby Monterey offers one of the world's finest public aquariums.*

The Point Pinos dwelling and tower reflect the rather incongruous Cape Cod–style architecture of California's first lighthouses.

POINT SUR LIGHT

Big Sur – 1889

For those who love natural beauty, the stretch of California Route 1 from San Simeon to Monterey ranks among the wonders of the world. Here the continent has thrown up a wall separating its desert valleys from the Pacific. Often hundreds of feet above the pounding surf, the narrow highway clings precariously to the escarpment of the Santa Lucia Mountains. Turnouts and roadside parks offer views usually available only to eagles or condors.

Located about thirty miles south of Monterey, the tiny town of Big Sur is a magnet for backpackers and nature-loving suburbanites. Timeless coastal redwoods hide here, protected from power saws by Pfeiffer State Park. Not nearly so old as the big trees, but nonetheless venerable, is the Point Sur Lighthouse, just to the north of the town. Established in 1889, the light warns sailors not to come too close to this dangerous coastline where mountains wrestle with the ocean.

The lighthouse stands at the summit of a steep-sided sandstone island connected to the mainland by a sandy causeway. Together with the 200-foot elevation of the hill, the fifty-foot stone tower places the light more than 250 feet above sea level.

Building the lighthouse atop the rugged hill proved challenging and expensive. Congress appropriated $50,000 for the project, but contractors spent that much and more. Before construction could move forward, a railroad track had to be laid to move materials to the site.

Once the lighthouse was completed and placed in operation, the tracks were removed, and the station could be reached only by climbing a staircase of 395 steps. Keepers developed strong leg muscles, especially since the station dwelling was located a considerable distance from the light tower. Later a tramway was installed, and eventually a winding roadway was cut through to the summit to make access easier.

HOW TO GET THERE: *The lighthouse is located off California Route 1 in Pfeiffer Big Sur State Park on a sharply elevated point near the town of Big Sur. Excellent views of the light can be had when traveling south along Highway 1 from Monterey and Carmel. For those who want a closer look, tours are available on Sundays. With its scenery, redwoods, hiking, and camping, nearby Big Sur is legendary. For information call the Point Sur State Historic Park at (831) 667–2315. The station's original first-order Fresnel lens is on display at the Allen Knight Maritime Museum in Monterey; call (831) 372–2608.*

(Courtesy Nancy A. Pizzo)

PIEDRAS BLANCAS LIGHT

San Simeon – 1875

The old Piedras Blancas Lighthouse appears decapitated, as if the wing of a low-flying airplane had chopped off its lantern. Indeed, the tower was once crowned by a handsome lantern, but it was lopped off the building in 1949 when the Coast Guard removed the station's first-order Fresnel lens and replaced it with a beacon much like those used at airports.

Completed in 1875, the cone-shaped brick tower once stood ninety feet tall on a grassy knoll that lifted its light 142 feet above sea level. Today, it is about twenty feet shorter. The modern-looking beacon seems out of place on the trunk of the old tower, but it boasts an extraordinary 1.4 million candlepower, making it visible from about eighteen miles at sea.

The Piedras Blancas beacon marks the halfway point between major coastal lights at Point Conception to the south and Pigeon Point to the north. The original lens, with its multiple bull's-eyes, is now proudly displayed in a small park beside California Route 1 in Cambria.

The station's fog signal, in operation since 1906, is one of the most powerful in the West. Its warning blasts are notoriously earsplitting.

HOW TO GET THERE: *The Piedras Blancas Light station is located off California Route 1 north of San Simeon. The views of the Pacific along this stretch of highway are truly extraordinary. Access to the lighthouse, however, is currently restricted. Visitors to the area may be astonished by the large gathering of elephant seals on the beaches near the lighthouse.*

The Piedras Blancas Lighthouse was impressive before it was turned into an ugly duckling by automation. The lantern room was removed in 1949, an act that, in effect, decapitated the structure.

SAN LUIS OBISPO LIGHT

San Luis Obispo – 1890

lthough the lovely old Spanish town of San Luis Obispo had a busy port and one of the best harbors in southern California, no lighthouse was built here in 1890. Regional political squabbling fueled by fierce competition with other coastal communities repeatedly blocked efforts to win congressional appropriations for a lighthouse. Finally, in the late 1880s, funds were made available. Construction began in 1888, but the station was not completed until two years later. At last, on the evening of June 30, 1890, the lamp was lit, and the lighthouse began the first of its almost ninety years of service.

Built on an isolated point on the west side of San Luis Obispo Bay, the two-story lighthouse was distinctly Victorian in design. A forty-foot square tower rose from a corner of the building and, together with the elevation of the point, placed the light more than 130 feet above the Pacific. The original optic was a fourth-order Fresnel lens. There was also a fog signal consisting of a ten-inch steam whistle.

Because there was no road leading to the point,

supplies had to be brought in by boat. Lighthouse Service supply steamers made regular calls at the San Luis Obispo station.

The light was automated in 1974, and two years later, the old lighthouse lost its job to a new cylindrical structure built just to the east of the original facility. The new tower boasts a pair of powerful, rotating airport-type beacons. The fourth-order Fresnel lens that served so long in the lighthouse has been moved to a museum in town. Local historical and conservation groups plan to restore the lighthouse and, in time, open it to the public.

HOW TO GET THERE: *Since the lighthouse is located near the Diablo Canyon Nuclear Power Plant, it has long been off limits to visitors. However, it is occasionally open for tours; call (805) 929–3847. The station's Fresnel lens can now be seen at the San Luis Obispo County Historical Museum at 696 Monterey Street, San Luis Obispo, CA 93406; (805) 543–0638. The museum is open from 10:00 A.M. to 4:00 P.M. Wednesday through Sunday.*

(Courtesy Nancy A. Pizzo)

The San Luis Obispo Lighthouse as it looked a century ago. The station was built in 1890 on the brow of a rugged headland about 130 feet above the Pacific. (Courtesy National Archives)

POINT ARGUELLO LIGHT

Point Arguello – 1901 AND 1934

For much of its 840-mile length, the coast of California runs in a generally north-south direction. But at Point Arguello, about 250 miles south of San Francisco, it angles sharply toward the east. Then, at Point Conception, only a dozen miles or so farther along, it turns again, this time running almost due east. Together, the two points form an elbow jutting far out into the Pacific. Swirling air currents sweeping over the points give them some of the most unpredictable and, occasionally, violent weather in the West.

Over the centuries, countless ships, their masters blinded by fog or storms, have misjudged the points and slammed into one of them. Among the vessels lost here were the seven doomed destroyers mentioned in the introduction to this chapter. So threatening is the angular geography here that officials chose Point Conception for one of the first lighthouses in the West, completed in 1856. It was almost half a century later, however, that Point Arguello, the most westward and prominent of the two features, also received a light.

Completed in February 1901, the Point Arguello station featured a fourth-order Fresnel lens displayed from atop a squat twenty-eight-foot tower. The elevation of the cliffs helped place the light almost one hundred feet above the waves, however. A powerful compressed-air fog siren was sounded whenever the point was "socked in." Ironically, neither the light nor the fog signal could save the passenger steamer *Santa Rosa*, which ran aground in 1911 only a couple of miles from the station. Nor did they prevent the destruction of Captain Watson's destroyer squadron at nearby Honda in 1923.

Isolated and difficult to supply, Point Arguello was among the first Pacific coast lights to be automated. Decommissioned in 1934, the lighthouse was razed and replaced by an airport-type beacon atop an iron skeleton tower. A radio beacon was placed on the point to assist the light in guiding mariners. Both remain in operation today.

HOW TO GET THERE: *Located on Vandenburg Air Force Base, Point Arguello is closed to the public. The best way to see it is from the sea. Rail passengers riding past Point Arguello, however, may catch a glimpse of this remote and rather unglamorous light station.*

(Courtesy National Archives)

This rather romantic early twentieth-century depiction of Point Conception shows a fog bell being pulled to the cliff-top lighthouse by a team of oxen. (Courtesy National Archives)

POINT CONCEPTION LIGHT

Point Conception – 1856 AND 1882

California has an elbow known as Point Conception. Here, ocean currents collide to produce some of America's worst coastal weather. Some mariners consider it to be a North American version of South America's infamous Cape Horn, where gales howl in the faces of sailors trying desperately to round it.

Spanish ships sailing westward out of the Pacific were always glad to see the point after months at sea, but it did not always offer them an amiable welcome. The ocean floor off Point Conception is littered with the remains of vessels from American, Spanish, and many other nation's ports. It is not known how many ships have gone down in the waters off the point. Many of them simply disappeared, leaving no trace and no one to mourn their crews except their wives, families, and friends, who watched for them in vain.

Aware of the point's nightmarish reputation, government officials selected it as a site for one of the West's first lighthouses. Construction of the tower and keeper's dwelling began in 1854, but the station was not in operation until 1856.

The contractors hired to build the lighthouse had great difficulty getting materials to the isolated point. Once the structure was complete, inspectors found the workmanship shoddy—the mortar between the bricks was already crumbling. What was worse, the tower was obviously too small to accommodate the first-order Fresnel lens and lighting apparatus purchased for the lantern. The contractors were forced to tear down the building and start over again, this time, no doubt, using better-quality mortar.

Meanwhile, there were delays in shipping the station's huge lens from Europe. For months the new lighthouse stood empty. When keeper George Parkinson arrived, he discovered that not only was his lighthouse without a lens, but a band of Indians had set up camp in the building. Employing a combination of threats, salty language, and other forms of persuasion, Parkinson was eventually able to evict the squatters.

In September 1855 the lamp and lens arrived by schooner, but several key parts were missing. They were not located for several months, and the keeper had to wait until February 1856 before he could finally display his light.

Parkinson and later keepers found the isolated Point Conception Lighthouse a "hardship" duty station. The nearest markets and stores were in Santa Barbara, more than sixty miles away, causing Parkinson to complain that the cost of shipping in supplies amounted to more than his government salary.

In 1875 Parkinson noticed a series of large cracks opening in the tower walls. Perhaps, after all, the construction work had not been solid. After an inspection team visited the site, the Lighthouse Board decided to abandon the structure and build another lighthouse about one hundred feet lower in elevation than the first. By locating the light lower on the point, they hoped to avoid the low-hanging clouds that had frequently obscured its predecessor.

Obviously, the second Point Conception Lighthouse was better built than the first. Completed in 1882, the fifty-two-foot tower still stands and still guides mariners with its flashing light. The station's original first-order Fresnel lens remains in operation.

The Point Conception Lighthouse is inaccessible to the public.

(Courtesy Bob and Sandra Shanklin)

Ocean blue, red tile roof, and green palm fronds complement the white walls of the Point Vicente Lighthouse near Los Angeles. The station is said to have a resident ghost, a lady who appears only on foggy nights.

CHAPTER FOUR

LIGHTS OF THE GOLDEN SHORES
Southern California

t should come as no surprise that lighthouses seem to be prime real estate for ghosts. That may be true in part because so many lighthouses—western ones in particular—are Victorian in style, giving them just the sort of look we often associate with the spectral and with things that go bump in the night. And because of their exposed locations, lighthouses certainly have more than their share of dark and stormy weather. Whether Victorian or not, the old, abandoned dwellings and tall towers, with their glowing lights, do have a distinctly ghostly feeling about them. Most are, in fact, quite old—a century or more—and have seen many generations of keepers. When stories are told about the keepers and the families who served at these isolated stations years ago, it is easy to imagine their spirits returning to haunt the places where they lived and worked so long.

THE LADY OF POINT VICENTE

More than one keeper of the Point Vicente Lighthouse has felt a chill run up and down his spine at night—especially when the station's ladylike ghost puts in an appearance. As with most lighthouse ghosts, this one is associated with a tragic story. According to legend, the lady's lover had drowned in a shipwreck, and she walked the grounds of the light station incessantly, waiting for him to rejoin her.

For decades, it seemed, the faithful lady drifted over the station grounds, sometimes almost nightly. Keepers and visitors would look out across the station property and there she would be, an indistinct shape floating just above the ground. Some said she wore a flowing white gown.

Unlike many other ghost stories, however, the Point Vicente apparition was not *all* talk and fantasy. The keepers swore they were really seeing something and were not—heaven forbid—drinking on duty. As it turns out, the keepers' eyes had not completely deceived them. The ghost stories may have been the work of their imaginations—lighthouse keeping is a lonely job—but what they were seeing was real enough.

The mystery was solved by a young assistant keeper with an exceptionally quick and skeptical mind. He took careful note of the lady's habits. She appeared only at night and most often when the station's powerful rotating beacon moved in her direction. She had a particular fondness for nights when there was a light fog.

The Point Vicente assistant keeper and amateur detective concluded that the feminine ghost was the work of slight imperfections in the third-order Fresnel lens in the lantern room atop the sixty-seven-foot tower. As the lens rotated, it refracted light toward the ground in a confusion of arcs. If the refractions came together in just the right way and found a patch of fog, the "lady" appeared. Despite the sensibleness of this explanation, most visitors prefer to believe a ghostly lady still walks the station grounds. And perhaps she does.

CALIFORNIA'S GHOST LIGHTHOUSES

Some lighthouses are themselves ghosts. After serving faithfully for decades—sometimes a hundred years or more—they were abandoned and allowed to fall into ruin. Other outmoded or no-longer-needed lighthouses were intentionally razed to make room for new government structures. Still others were sold as surplus property into private hands for use as yacht clubs, restaurants, and storage houses. California has more than its share of "ghost" lighthouses, historic structures that now exist only in memory.

Southern California

A two-story, Victorian-style wooden structure with an attached tower, the Ballast Point Lighthouse served San Diego Bay for nearly seventy years. Erected in 1890, it was torn down in 1960 to make way for a U.S. Navy submarine base. The station was known to many for its lovely palms, planted during the 1940s by keeper Radford Franke. A small automated light still burns at Ballast Point today, but the lighthouse and palm trees are gone.

Although a lighthouse still stands on Point Heuneme in Oxnard, and its light still guides ships, an earlier lighthouse that stood here is remembered more fondly by some local old-timers. A gracious Victorian building, it was a twin of the beautiful lighthouse that survives to this day on Point Fermin. Built in 1874, the original Point Heuneme Lighthouse was placed in service on December 15 of that same year, as was its sister, Point Fermin Light. After more than sixty years of service, the Point Heuneme Lighthouse was removed to make way for widening and dredging the shipping

Built in a Victorian style in 1890, the Ballast Point Lighthouse guided vessels into San Diego's Harbor until 1960, when it was torn down to make way for a submarine base. (Courtesy U.S. Coast Guard)

channel just off the point. Sold into private hands for use as a yacht club, it was allowed to fall into disrepair and was eventually torn down.

The old and prosperous Spanish mission community of Santa Barbara received one of the first U.S. lighthouses built on the West Coast. A Cape Cod–style dwelling with a cylindrical tower rising through its roof, the Santa Barbara Lighthouse served mariners for nearly three-quarters of a century before it was destroyed in a major earthquake in 1925.

Central California

While a powerful light and radio beacon still guides ships safely around Point Arguello, the lighthouse built here at the turn of the twentieth century is long gone. The Coast Guard razed the building to minimize maintenance costs. Seven U.S. Navy destroyers ran aground near the lighthouse in 1923.

Perhaps the most ghostly of California's abandoned light stations is the one on Año Nuevo Island off the central coast north of Monterey. The tower has fallen over on its side and, together with other crumbling buildings, lies in a jumble among the island rocks. The scene suggests an ancient ruin, and seals and seabirds treat the place as if it had never been touched by human hands. Established in 1872, the station had a fog signal but no lighthouse until 1890, when a lantern was mounted atop a water tank. A skeleton tower with a Fresnel lens was placed here in 1915. The Año Nuevo Island Lighthouse was the first duty station for a young Radford Franke, who later served for many years at the Ballast Point Lighthouse. The station was closed in 1948.

Now a wave-swept ruin, the Ano Nuevo Island Lighthouse looked like this during its operational years (1872–1948). (Courtesy U.S. Coast Guard)

San Francisco Bay

The Point Knox Lighthouse on Angel Island in San Francisco Bay was the duty station of a legendary female keeper named Juliet Nichols. She was the widow of Captain Henry Nichols, who had served as Inspector of California Lighthouses before being killed in the Philippines during the Spanish-American War. From 1902 until she retired in 1914, Juliet Nichols kept the Point Knox light burning and its fog bell ringing. On one foggy day, when the signal's automatic striker was out of service, she rang the bell by hand for more than twenty hours. The light and fog signal were shifted to nearby Point Blunt in 1961. The unused Point Knox Lighthouse burned down in 1973.

In 1890 Oakland received a small lighthouse with a fifth-order Fresnel lens to guide vessels in and out of its bustling harbor. Much of the harbor traffic was due to the immense volume of passengers and freight arriving in Oakland by rail over the transcontinental line. Built on pilings at the end of a two-mile-long pier, the Oakland Harbor Lighthouse guided shipping and warned vessels away from the pier. For fog and heavy weather, it had a 3,500-pound bell that rang out at five-second intervals. When the station was automated in 1966, the lighthouse building was sold and shipped away for use as a restaurant.

In 1905 a small light station was placed on Southhampton Shoal near Oakland, in order to protect ferries plowing back and forth across the bay. A squared-off, two-story structure with gables, it stood on piles directly over the shoal. When the station was automated in 1960, the building was sold for use as a yacht club.

A small wooden lighthouse once served the navy's Pacific Fleet on Mare Island, near the junctions of the Sacramento, San Joaquin, and Napa Rivers. The two-story, Victorian-style structure was completed and in service by 1873. Among those who kept the Mare Island Light was Kate McDougal, widow of Commander D. J. McDougal, an inspector of lighthouses. Commander McDougal drowned while trying to land at Point Pinos to inspect the lighthouse there. It is said the inspector fell into the sea and was dragged down by the weight of the gold and silver coins he was

The Oakland Harbor Lighthouse once stood at the end of a long pier, reaching far out into San Francisco Bay. Nowadays, it's a restaurant. (Courtesy Bob and Sandra Shanklin)

Replaced by an automated beacon in 1951, the Carquinez Lighthouse was sold and eventually became an office for a popular marina. (Courtesy Bob and Sandra Shanklin)

carrying to pay the Point Pinos keepers. Mrs. McDougal's career as keeper spanned more than thirty years. The lovely old lighthouse where she lived and worked was abandoned in 1917 and torn down a few years later.

Built in 1890 and lit early in 1891, the Roe Island Lighthouse guarded a bank of dangerous shallows on the north side of the channel through Suisan Bay. Its fixed white light was provided by a fifth-order Fresnel lens. An ornate wooden structure with a lantern perched on its roof, the lighthouse was severely damaged by the World War II–era explosion of an ammunition shipping facility at nearby Port Chicago. The force of the 1944 blast wrecked the station's fog-bell house, shattered windows, and cracked walls. The damage was never repaired, and the station was closed in 1945. It was later destroyed by fire.

Beginning in 1910 Carquinez Strait Lighthouse guided vessels into the narrow passage connecting the San Pablo and Suisan Bays. It was construction of this station that led to the abandonment of the Mare Island Lighthouse. The Carquinez Strait Light burned until 1951, when the station was replaced by an automated beacon and fog signal positioned on the end of the pier. Sold to a private owner and moved to Vallejo on a barge, the lighthouse was converted for use as marina offices.

Northern California

Among California's earliest lights, the Humboldt Lighthouse near Eureka was completed in 1856. Built on a sandy foundation, the building was never stable. The Cape Cod–style lighthouse was very nearly destroyed by a powerful earthquake in 1877. Over time, beach erosion completed the destruction by undermining the building's weak foundation. Replaced by the Table Bluff Lighthouse in 1892, the venerable structure eventually collapsed into a jumble of masonry. Bits and pieces of the old lighthouse can still be found on the beach.

SANTA BARBARA LIGHT

Santa Barbara – 1856

One of the West Coast's earliest light stations, the Santa Barbara Lighthouse began operation in 1856. A relatively modest structure with a light tower rising through the center of the keeper's dwelling, it was much less costly than some of its cousins elsewhere along the Pacific coast. Builder George Nagle of San Francisco received only $8,000 for completing the project—compared to the more than $38,000 bill for the Tatoosh Island (Cape Flattery) light built at about the same time.

Despite its bargain-basement price tag, the lighthouse served faithfully for nearly three-quarters of a century. Then, during the early summer of 1925, its career came to a sudden, rude end when a powerful earthquake shook many buildings in Santa Barbara to their foundations. When the quake struck, shortly before dawn on June 29, the keeper was asleep. But he quickly understood what was happening and herded his family outside. They reached safety just before the structure collapsed, throwing up a large cloud of masonry dust.

The old lighthouse, along with its fourth-order Fresnel lens, was completely destroyed by the quake. The station's light burned from atop a temporary wooden tower while it was being rebuilt.

One of the West's most famous lighthouse keepers was a woman. Beginning in 1865 Mrs. Julia Williams kept the Santa Barbara light for more than forty years. It is said she was away from her duties only two nights during her entire career as keeper. Her faithfulness did not prevent her from raising five children, all of whom grew up in the lighthouse.

The Santa Barbara Lighthouse as it appeared during the early twentieth century. It was destroyed by an earthquake in 1925. (Courtesy National Archives)

POINT HUENEME LIGHT

Oxnard – 1874 AND 1941

ollowing the gold rush, shipping along the southern California coast increased steadily, bringing with it demands for lights to mark important channels and navigational hazards. The need for a light to guide ships through heavily trafficked and often dangerous Santa Barbara Channel was considered especially urgent. The channel and the mountainous islands that formed its outer wall had claimed many ships, including the hapless passenger steamer *Winfield Scott,* wrecked on Anacapa Island in 1853.

Since the Channel Islands were thought to be far too rugged to allow construction of a light station, government officials decided to establish one on the mainland instead. The site selected for the new lighthouse was Point Hueneme, which thrusts seaward from Ventura, near the eastern entrance of the channel. Low in elevation and difficult to see from the water, the point was considered a threat to ships. The new light was thus able to serve the dual purpose of guarding the point and guiding vessels in and out of the channel.

The original Point Hueneme Lighthouse was an ornate, Victorian-style structure with a square, fifty-two-foot wood-and-brick tower rising through its pitched roof. The unusual design was identical to that of a sister station at Point Fermin in Los Angeles. Both lighthouses were completed in 1874, and both were first lit on December of that year. Each of them was given a fourth-order Fresnel lens. The Point Hueneme station displayed a flashing white light, while the light at Point Fermin flashed white and red alternately.

The Point Hueneme light can still be seen, but the beautiful old lighthouse is long gone. Razed shortly before World War II to make way for a major channel-dredging operation, it was replaced by a square, concrete tower about fifty feet tall. Fitted with the station's original optics, the blocky, buff-colored tower served just as effectively as its predecessor but had little to recommend it as a work of architecture. The light continues to serve seagoing traffic entering Point Hueneme, which attracts considerable commerical traffic and support vessels for offshore rigs.

HOW TO GET THERE: *The tower is located on an active naval installation and is off limits to visitors. The lighthouse can be seen from a path leading north from the Hueneme fishing pier. The light itself can be seen from Point Hueneme and many points along the nearby coast.*

Point Hueneme Lighthouse, as it appeared prior to World War I.

(Courtesy U.S. Coast Guard)

ANACAPA ISLAND LIGHT

Anacapa Island – 1912 AND 1932

ong ago, the Channel Islands off the coast of south central California were home to an extraordinary race of pygmy mammoths. Unlike their giant, elephantlike cousins on the mainland, these mammoths were dwarves, little larger than ponies. No one is sure how the ancestors of these unusual creatures reached the island chain or why they went there. Scientists can only assume that mammoths occasionally swam across the channel—one much narrower than today—for reasons now lost in the mists of natural history. When ocean levels rose at the end of the Ice Age, the channel widened dramatically, marooning a herd of full-sized mammoths on the islands. Although grazing was very poor and living conditions harsh, the herd survived for thousands of years. Adapting to the limitations of their island environment, the mammoths grew smaller, generation by generation, achieving diminutive stature. In time the island mammoths died out or were killed off by seafaring Native American hunters, who found them easy to kill with spears. All that remains of the little mammoths today are their bones.

A more fortunate band of castaways were the 250 passengers and crew of the steamer *Winfield Scott,* which set out from San Francisco late in 1853, bound

for Panama. Many of those on board had already proven they were the lucky sort, having recently struck it rich in the California goldfields. Now they were headed back home to enjoy their newfound wealth, but on the night of December 2, their golden luck almost ran out. Lost in a thick blanket of fog, the *Winfield Scott* plowed into Anacapa Island and sank. Incredibly, everyone aboard managed to scramble through the surf to safety.

Some stumbled ashore dragging hefty bags of gold dust, but in these circumstances, their glittering riches could buy them little comfort. Several weeks passed before their plight was known and help arrived. Meanwhile, the survivors lived in desperate privation, huddled in crude shelters made from bits and pieces of wreckage. They had practically no food or water, and by the time they were finally rescued, they had almost starved. The few eggs they managed to steal from birds' nests became literally worth their weight in gold.

The *Winfield Scott* was only one of countless vessels torn apart by the merciless rocks of the islands, which, in fact, were the exposed summits of a rugged, underwater mountain range. There had been many earlier wrecks here, such as that of the Spanish treasure ship *San Sebastian,* lost in 1784 along with a large shipment of gold doubloons. There were many later wrecks as well—traffic along the California coast increased sharply during the prosperous era that followed the gold rush. But while maritime interests and government officials recognized the crying need for a light to warn ships, construction of a lighthouse on the precipitous island cliffs was thought to be next to impossible. A new century had dawned before this daunting and expensive project was undertaken. Although a substitute mainland light station was placed on nearby Point Hueneme in 1874, it could do little to guard the islands themselves.

Finally, in 1912, an iron skeleton tower was built on Anacapa Island at the eastern entrance of the channel, not far from where the *Winfield Scott* had come to grief more than half a century earlier. The tower's acetylene

(Courtesy Bob and Sandra Shanklin)

lamp was tended periodically by keepers who crossed from Ventura on the mainland.

Not until 1932 was a permanent, fully staffed light station established on the island. Its centerpiece was a handsome, cylindrical masonry tower complete with a third-order Fresnel lens. Standing on the island's highest point, the thirty-nine-foot tower placed its light more than 275 feet above the ocean, from which height it could be seen by mariners more than twenty-five miles away. The station's diaphonic fog signals were among the most powerful in the West and could be heard from up to a dozen miles at sea. Dwellings and other support structures stood down on the shore, and keepers had to climb hundreds of steps every morning and evening to tend the light.

Supplies were brought in by boat, but providing water for station personnel on the arid island was a continual problem. An enormous catchment basin covering some 30,000 square feet yielded an average of only about fifty gallons per day. Tenders delivered supplemental supplies from the mainland, storing up to 50,000 gallons in a pair of redwood tanks.

Water became less of a concern when the station was automated in 1966 and its full-time staff moved on to duties elsewhere. The original Fresnel lens was replaced by an airport-style beacon in 1990. Today, the lighthouse is part of the Channel Islands National Park, which, with its seals, seabirds, and extraordinary scenery, is one of the nation's foremost natural treasures. Nowadays, except when excited park visitors cross the channel from Ventura, the lighthouse stands its vigil alone. Each night and always in fog or foul weather, it faithfully marks the entrance to the Santa Barbara Channel. Should any woolly mammoth attempt to swim over from the mainland today, it would have a light to follow.

HOW TO GET THERE: *The scenic wonders of the Channel Islands National Park provide a lovely frame for one of the West's most beautiful lighthouses. Visits to Anacapa and other islands are available through park concessionaires in Ventura. For schedules or to arrange a trip, call Island Packer Cruises and Boats at (805) 642–1393. A stop at park headquarters, located on the harbor in Ventura, is highly recommended. Films and exhibits at the headquarters provide insight into the island's natural history as well as its likely future. For additional information contact Channel Island National Park, 1901 Spinnaker Drive, Ventura, CA 93001; (805) 658-5730.*

(Courtesy U.S. Coast Guard)

A U.S. Coast Guard crewman takes measurements inside the lantern at the Anacapa Island Lighthouse off the southern California coast. The station's bull's-eye Fresnel lens nearly fills the room. (Courtesy U.S. Goast Guard)

POINT VICENTE LIGHT

Rancho Palos Verdes – **1926**

Point Vicente Lighthouse not only has one of the world's most beautiful settings but even its own resident ghost (see the introduction to this chapter). It should thus come as no surprise that, located only a few miles from Hollywood, this classically styled lighthouse has been featured in dozens of movies and television series' episodes.

Perched atop reddish brown cliffs that drop more than one hundred feet into the azure Pacific, the white cylinder of the Point Vicente tower presents a photogenic image from almost any angle. For mariners, however, it looks best at night, when its 1.1-million-candlepower beacon warns ships away from the ragged point and its deadly rocks. Among the most prominent coastal features in southern California, Point Vicente threatens vessels swinging eastward from the open Pacific toward San Pedro Harbor at Los Angeles Harbor. An array of rocks several hundred yards offshore add to the danger.

Despite the prominence of the point and its threat to navigation, no light was placed here until well into the twentieth century. Built in 1926, the masonry tower stands sixty-seven feet tall. Its extraordinarily powerful light can be seen from twenty miles at sea.

The lantern room is still graced by its original third-order Fresnel lens. It displays a flashing light every twenty seconds. During World War II, the Fresnel was temporarily replaced by a small lighting apparatus that could be more easily blacked out during an air or sea raid.

HOW TO GET THERE: *The Point Vicente Light station is located north of Marineland off Palos Verdes Drive West in Rancho Palos Verdes. A drive along Hawthorne Boulevard (California 107) provides fine views of the light, which can also be seen from the Interpretive Center at 31501 Palos Verdes Drive. Near the lighthouse itself, the center offers a wealth of information about the light and the scenic Palos Verdes Peninsula. For information call (310) 377–5370.*

As this beautiful scene illustrates, California is a land of rich colors and stark contrasts. Built on one of the loveliest sites in California, the Point Vicente Lighthouse guides vessels headed for the busy San Pedro Harbor.

POINT FERMIN LIGHT
Los Angeles – 1874

No longer functional, the Point Fermin Lighthouse remains a venerable landmark. It was built in 1874 from lumber and brick shipped around the tip of South America. Its ornate gingerbread design is unique among American lighthouses.

HOW TO GET THERE: *Refurbished and maintained by preservationists because of its historical* *and architectural merit, the 1874 Point Fermin Lighthouse is the centerpiece of a Los Angeles city park. The redwood Victorian building is occupied by a park employee and is closed to the public. Located on Paseo Del Mar, west of Pacific Avenue, the park offers an excellent place to view the Los Angeles Harbor Lighthouse.*

For more than a century this handsome Victorian structure has graced Point Fermin, now a Los Angeles city park. The building has such a homey appearance that some park visitors are unaware it is a lighthouse. (Photo by Kim Andrews)

Generations of photographers, artists, and sightseers have been attracted to Point Fermin by its spectacular scenery. This 1893 photograph shows the Point Fermin Lighthouse perched on a cliff far above the Pacific. (Courtesy U.S. Coast Guard)

LOS ANGELES HARBOR LIGHT

Los Angeles – 1913

As classical in appearance as its Long Beach neighbor is unconventional, the Los Angeles Harbor Lighthouse anchors the far end of the San Pedro Breakwater. Having weathered countless gales, stood through more than one earthquake, and even survived a brush with a U.S. Navy battleship, the tower leans out of plumb but remains solid and functional.

HOW TO GET THERE: *Somewhat resembling a column on a Greek temple, the Los Angeles Harbor Lighthouse is located at the end of the harbor breakwater east of Pacific Avenue at Paseo Del Mar. It can be seen from Pacific Avenue and from the city park at Point Fermin, where visitors can also enjoy the Point Fermin Lighthouse.*

Located at the end of the San Pedro Harbor Breakwater, the Los Angeles Lighthouse rises more than seventy feet above water.

LONG BEACH HARBOR LIGHT

Los Angeles – 1949

Standing three blocky-concrete stories above the San Pedro Middle Breakwater in Los Angeles, the Long Beach Harbor Light is a very strange-looking edifice. Its appearance suggests one of those lumbering robots in a low-budget science fiction movie of the sort made during the 1940s and 1950s. Concrete columns provide the structure with legs, a bulky rectangular platform gives it a body, and a squared-off upper story serves as a head. A pair of foghorns could be mistaken for eyes, and an iron superstructure sits atop the head like an enormous hat or helmet.

Completed more than half a century ago, the Long Beach Harbor Light was built at a time when architects thought in terms of modernism and the purely functional. It marked a radical departure from tradition and was the furthest thing imaginable from an old-fashioned lighthouse with a cylindrical tower and Cape Cod–style dwelling. Designed to withstand both earthquakes and high winds, it was supported by six cylindrical columns made of cement cast into huge molds. Since the light was completely automated from the first, there was never any need for a keeper's dwelling.

When the light went into operation in 1949, the forty-two-foot-high rectangular tower became the focus of considerable media attention because of its robotlike appearance and automated capabilities. Considered the very image of modernity, the undecorated edifice was immediately dubbed the "robot light." Actually, it was not a robot at all; rather, its functions were monitored and controlled electronically from the nearby Los Angeles Lighthouse. Nowadays, computers keep tabs on light and relay commands to its airport-style beacon.

The technology that made possible this rather severely practical lighthouse is now passé, so it has little to recommend it as a landmark. Nonetheless, it continues to do its job each night in a workmanlike, if not robotic, fashion. More than one weary mariner, anxious to avoid slamming into the breakwater, has been exceptionally happy to see it. And to this day, the light remains very popular with children, who may recognize a friendly face in its cartoonlike features.

HOW TO GET THERE: *Located at the end of the Middle San Pedro Breakwater, the Long Beach Lighthouse cannot be reached easily from shore. Its light can be seen, however, from numerous points along the coast.*

Ultramodern even by today's standards, the Long Beach Harbor Lighthouse looks a bit like a space invader from a 1950s science fiction movie. Los Angeles children sometimes call it "the Robot Light."

(Courtesy Bob and Sandra Shanklin)

LIGHTHOUSES OF POINT LOMA

Old Point Loma – 1855

Point Loma – 1891

The history of navigational markers on Point Loma runs from Spanish times, when residents of San Diego built fires here to help royal supply ships find the harbor. Following the acquisition of California by the United States, the government undertook to erect lighthouses to help guide ships along the nation's now-lengthy western seaboard. Among these was the Old Point Loma Lighthouse, built atop the same hill where the Spanish signal fires had once burned.

Construction began in the spring of 1854 but was not completed until November of the following year. For materials, builders used locally quarried sandstone and brick brought by ship from Monterey.

The cost of the project amounted to $30,000, considerably more than had been budgeted. What was worse, once the structure was built, it quickly became apparent that Uncle Sam had not gotten all he had paid for. A first-order Fresnel lens had been ordered for the station, but when it arrived, try as they might, builders could not fit it into the lantern—the lighthouse was too small to accommodate it. Rather than tear down the building and start over, they substituted the less powerful, third-order lens meant for the Humboldt Harbor Lighthouse on the northern California coast. Eventually, the big first-order lens ended up at the Cape Flattery Lighthouse, far to the north of its intended home.

Despite the smaller lens, the Point Loma Light proved very powerful indeed. Mariners could usually see it from twenty-five miles away, but some sea captains claimed to have spotted the light from a distance of nearly forty miles. The news was not all good, however. All too often clouds and fog obscured the light.

When Point Loma had been surveyed, it had seemed the perfect site for a lighthouse. Not only was it well positioned at the entrance of San Diego Harbor, it also offered an impressive elevation of more than 460 feet. This height made it the lofti-

The "Old" Point Loma Lighthouse is well named. It was among the first lighthouses built on America's West Coast. Construction began in 1854 and was completed the following year.

est lighthouse in America but in time would also lead to its demise as an active light station. As it turned out, the elevation of the lighthouse frequently placed it above low-lying cloud banks. In heavy weather, when the light was most needed, mariners often could not see it at all.

So in 1891, thirty-six years after its lamps were first lit, the Old Point Loma Light went dark. The New Point Loma Lighthouse, built at a lower, more practical, elevation, took over its duties, and the venerable structure fell into disuse and decay. In 1913 it survived an abortive attempt to demolish it and replace it with an enormous statue of a Spanish explorer. Then, in 1933, it was rescued from ruin, renovated, and made part of the Cabrillo National Monument. As the monument's chief attraction, the lighthouse draws many thousands of visitors each year.

HOW TO GET THERE: *The Point Loma lighthouses are the primary attractions of Cabrillo National Monument in San Diego. To reach the monument and lighthouses, follow Route 209 to the end of Point Loma. The old Cape Cod–style lighthouse, out of service since 1891, stands near the crest of the point, several hundred feet above the sea. Far below, at the edge of the Pacific, stands the iron-skeleton tower that took over the work of the original lighthouse more than a century ago. Operated as a museum by the National Park Service, the Old Point Loma Lighthouse is open to the public, but its hardworking neighbor is not. Yet an excellent view of the "new" Point Loma Lighthouse can be enjoyed from the road to the monument's famed tidal pools. Point Loma is a good place to watch whales during their annual southward migration in the winter. For more information on Cabrillo National Monument, call (619) 557–5450.*

The iron-skeleton Point Loma Lighthouse replaced its more lofty ancestor in 1891. Although it could hardly be described as an architectural wonder, it continues to serve mariners today, more than a century after its construction. Its third-order Fresnel lens lights the way into San Diego Harbor.

The 138-foot Kalaupapa tower is the tallest lighthouse in Hawaii. Located on an isolated peninsula, it warns vessels away from Molokai's northern sea cliffs. (Courtesy Bob and Sandra Shanklin)

CHAPTER FIVE

LIGHTS OF THE ALOHA ISLANDS

Hawaii

I ronically, the Pacific, the world's greatest ocean, floats atop a vast lake of fiery magma. The Pacific floor consists of a fragile layer of basalt barely thick enough to separate the ocean's cold, deep waters from the molten rock just below. Occasionally, the basalt buckles and cracks open, bringing seawater into contact with the magma and touching off one of nature's most violent spectacles—a volcanic eruption. Such events can be tremendously destructive, unleashing powerful earthquakes and launching tsunamis capable of devastating coastlines thousands of miles away. But they are also prodigiously creative. The Hawaiian Islands owe their very existence to a series of such eruptions that began millions of years ago.

Hawaii is located over a planetary "hot spot" where mysterious currents welling up from the earth's super-heated interior produce intense volcanic activity. The almost continuous eruptions generated by the hot spot spew enormous quantities of lava into the sea. Cooled by the water, the molten rock quickly solidifies to form first an undersea mountain, then a volcanic cone above the surface, and finally an extensive island.

As is the case with all continental plates, this part of the Pacific seafloor is constantly in motion, and it drifts northwestward at a rate of a few inches each year. In time, this slow-moving conveyor belt will shift a once highly active volcanic island off the hot spot. Eventually, the island's volcanoes grow cold and its mountains erode until finally nothing is left but a sandy atoll. Meanwhile, the hot spot creates new islands to the southeast of the old one. Over a period of seventy million years, this process has built a chain of mid-Pacific islands and atolls more than 3,000 miles long.

A LIGHT TOWER AS TALL AS EVEREST

Currently, the most active of the archipelago's fiery volcanic cinder cones are located on the Island of Hawaii, known to most locals as the "Big Island." Their lava flows increase the size of the island by an average of five acres each year while adding to the colossal bulk of Mauna Loa, Hawaii's mightiest volcano. More than 10,000 cubic miles of volcanic rock and ash deposited by uncounted thousands of eruptions have raised its summit to an altitude of 13,677 feet above sea level. Measured from its base on the seafloor, however, Mauna Loa soars more than 30,000 feet, making it even taller than Mount Everest.

For eons, the volcanic Hawaiian chain was nature's best-kept secret. Located more than 2,500 miles from the nearest landmass—North America—Hawaii developed unique flora and fauna. Birds were the only visitors from afar, and most of them might never have arrived had they not been blown off course by storms. For millions of years no human feet left prints in the golden sands of Hawaii's beaches. Then, about 1,700 years ago, the sails of voyaging canoes appeared on the horizon.

No one will ever know for sure how the first Polynesian settlers found these remote islands, but it is easy to imagine that Hawaii's lofty volcanoes played a role in the discovery. Perhaps Polynesian mariners sailing far to the northeast of Tahiti spotted the glow of a Mauna Loa eruption. Later, settlers might have sailed toward the glow as if following the beacon of a giant lighthouse.

CHICKENS, SWEET POTATOES, AND SIGNAL FIRES

Hawaii's first settlers brought staples with them in their twin-hulled canoes—taro, coconut, and sweet potato as well as pigs, dogs, and chickens—and with these they were able to make abundant lives for themselves in Hawaii. They established permanent communities, traded with one another, and fought wars for possession of this cove or that island. Likely as not, they traveled between the islands with the help of signal fires, Hawaii's first man-made navigational lights.

The islands would remain the Polynesian's alone for nearly two millennia. Hawaii remained largely unknown to westerners until Britain's Captain James Cook dropped anchor in Kealakekua Bay in 1778. Other explorers followed as did whaling vessels, merchant ships, and missionaries.

Prior to the arrival of westerners, Hawaii had been ruled by a hodgepodge of chiefs and strongmen with domains scattered throughout the islands. During the 1790s an ambitious chief named Kamehameha obtained cannon from an America ship and used them to conquer the entire Hawaiian chain. Kamehameha set himself up as king of Hawaii, establishing his royal capital at Lahaina on Maui. Western merchants and emissaries flocked to Lahaina to seek favors from Kamehameha and his descendants. After 1840 their vessels were guided by a lighthouse, the first in all of what would eventually become the western United States. From that time forward, lighthouses would play an important role in the history of Hawaii as a kingdom (until 1893), a republic (1894–1898), a U.S. territory (1898–1959), and a state (as of 1959).

Hawaii has long been heavily dependent on maritime commerce and remains so today. For this reason lighthouses are vital not just to those onboard the ships trying—sometimes desperately—to find these remote islands, but to the people and economy of Hawaii itself. Even today, in an age of sophisticated shipboard electronics, Hawaii's navigational lights remain important to mariners. At the very least, they make the job of navigators a little easier.

This chapter focuses on several of Hawaii's most remarkable lighthouses. Among these are the Makapuu Point Lighthouse with its extraordinarily large and powerful lens; the Kalaupapa Lighthouse with its haunted past; the Diamond Head Lighthouse, home to the commander of the Pacific District of the U.S. Coast Guard; the Kilauea Lighthouse, which serves now as a beacon for seabirds rather than ships; and the Lahaina Lighthouse, which still marks Hawaii's old royal capital.

MAKAPUU POINT LIGHT

East of Honolulu – 1909

All of the Hawaiian Islands together comprise less than 7,000 square miles of land. That may seem like a lot to a homeowner whose own plot of ground is likely less than an acre, but when compared to the vastness of the Pacific, it is infinitesimal. The islands are all but lost in the Pacific's seventy million square miles of blue water. Locating these relatively tiny specks of land has always been a concern for Pacific mariners as it is possible to sail right past without ever catching sight of them. To make it easier to find them, the U.S. government ringed the island chain with a necklace of sparkling navigational lights.

Prominent among these is the light on Makapuu Point, established in 1909. Built on the side of a cliff on Oahu, the most populous and commercially vital of all the islands, it points the way to bustling Honolulu.

The huge, twelve-foot-high Fresnel at Makapuu is the largest lighthouse lens in the United States. Ironically, it is housed in a small tower only thirty-five feet tall, but what the station lacks in stature it more than makes up in the power of its beacon—visible from more than twenty-eight miles at sea. Unlike the tower itself, the station's surroundings are Olympian in scale. When the Makapuu Lighthouse was built in the early twentieth century, workers had to blast a site from a solid wall of lava several hundred feet high. Perched on an artificial ledge more than three hundred feet above the waves, the stone and steel tower and its powerful lens still serve mariners.

HOW TO GET THERE: *Located off Highway 72 in the easternmost corner of Oahu, the lighthouse can be reached only by means of a strenuous uphill climb. Bring your hiking shoes.*

(Courtesy Bob and Sandra Shanklin)

DIAMOND HEAD LIGHT

Honolulu – 1899 AND 1917

athers splashing in the warm waters that wash Wakikiki's famed beaches can look over their shoulders at a looming wall of dark-colored rock and ash—the cone and crater of the extinct Diamond Head Volcano. The Hawaiian name for the crater is "Ring of Fire." Likely, the name refers not to the crater's volcanic origins but rather to the fact that early Hawaiians marked this prominent point with signal fires—even sturdy Polynesian mariners needed all the help they could get to locate the islands. Nowadays, the point possesses a somewhat more modern signal fire, namely, the Diamond Head Lighthouse.

Among the more scenic light stations anywhere, the Diamond Head Lighthouse is located on an active Coast Guard base and is, unfortunately, off limits to the public. Established in 1899, the station consists of a fifty-seven-foot square concrete tower and a wooden keeper's dwelling. The light tower had to be completely rebuilt after severe cracks appeared in its foundation. The new tower, completed in 1917, was given reinforced-concrete walls and fitted with the station's original third-order Fresnel lens. The existing dwelling dates from 1921.

Certainly among Hawaii's most important navigational aids, the Diamond Head Light guides vessels headed toward Honolulu, still the busiest port in the mid-Pacific. Essentially unchanged in more than eighty years, the lighthouse remains in operation, its automated beacon shining out over the ocean from an elevation of 147 feet. Nowadays, the station dwelling serves as residence for the commander of the U.S. Coast Guard 14th District.

HOW TO GET THERE: *Located southeast of Waikiki, the station is part of an active Coast Guard base and is not open to the public.*

The Diamond Head Lighthouse stands at the edge of an extinct volcano. At night, the lighthouse beacon points the way to Honolulu. (Courtesy Bob and Sandra Shanklin)

LAHAINA LIGHT

Lahaina on Maui – 1840 AND 1916

Having unified the islands through conquest during the 1790s, Hawaii's King Kamehameha I established his royal capital at Lahaina. Its harbor became an important port of call for diplomats, merchants, and missionaries, who came here to ask favors of Kamehameha and his descendants. Beginning in 1840, Lahaina's harbor was marked by a lighthouse, perhaps the first in all of what is now the western United States. Unfortunately, nothing is left of that early lighthouse, which was replaced in 1916 by the existing concrete tower. This simple, pyramidal structure still guides vessels in and out of the harbor with its modest beacon.

Rising from dockside in Lahaina's historic waterfront district, the thirty-nine-foot tower is located near the berth of *Carthaginian*, a replica of the supply schooners that served the Pacific whaling fleet during the mid-nineteenth century. A ladder on the outside of the tower provides access to the modern optical device at the top.

Today, because of its royal history and beautiful scenery, Lahaina attracts droves of tourists to its quaint streets. Ferry passengers approaching the area may get a good view of the tower and its light.

HOW TO GET THERE: *The tower is located just off Front Street near the center of Lahaina. Call (808) 667–9193.*

A simple, pyramidal tower marks Hawaii's old royal capital. (Courtesy Bob and Sandra Shanklin)

KALAUPAPA LIGHT
Kalaupapa Peninsula on Molokai – 1908

Once the site of a notorious leper colony, the Kalaupapa Peninsula on Molokai is backed by the highest sea cliffs in the world—some soaring more than 2,000 feet above the waves. To help mariners keep their distance from these rugged shores, the government established a lighthouse on Kalaupapa Point in 1908.

Kalaupapa's soaring octagonal tower dates to 1908. For many years, this light station shared the remote Kalaupapa Peninsula with a leper colony. (Courtesy Bob and Sandra Shanklin)

The exceptional remoteness of the peninsula made getting materials and construction crews to this faraway site unusually difficult and expensive. Building the station cost $60,000, but it has proven invaluable to mariners and their vessels. The 138-foot tower is the tallest on the Pacific.

The station and the nearby remains of a leper colony are now part of the Kalaupapa National Historical Park. The park reveals the tragic story of the colony and the patients condemned to live out their lives there. Hansen's disease, more often known as leprosy, apparently was brought to the islands by westerners, and native Hawaiians proved unusually susceptible to it. Since there was no cure for this dreaded, disfiguring disease, those who contracted it were isolated at Kalaupapa. Cut off from the rest of Hawaii by the towering cliffs and the churning Pacific, Kalaupapa was in essence a prison. When modern drugs proved effective against the disease, the policy of forced separation was discontinued. The last patients arrived at the colony in 1969.

HOW TO GET THERE: *Reaching the remote Kalaupapa Peninsula is not much easier today than it was a century ago as there is no direct road access. Some visitors climb down from the cliffs on foot or ride down on the backs of surefooted mules, but these options are not recommended for the faint of heart. Some flights are available. Contact Kalaupapa National Historical Park, Kalaupapa, Hawaii 96742. For tours call (808) 567–6171.*

KILAUEA POINT LIGHT

Kilauea Point on Kauai – 1913

stablished in 1913, the Kilauea Point Lighthouse guided several generations of mariners, its beacon focused by one of the largest clamshell lenses in the world. A light here still marks the far northwestern edge of the Hawaiian chain, but it no longer emanates from the lighthouse or the giant Fresnel that still graces its fifty-two-foot tower. Instead it shines from a much smaller structure nearby. The old lighthouse and lens are now a key attraction of the Kilauea Point National Wildlife Refuge, a natural wonderland alive with frigate birds, albatrosses, and other seabirds.

In 1927 the Kilauea Point Light helped guide a big mechanical bird to the islands. On June 28th pilot Lester "Lone Eagle" Maitland and his navigator Albert Hegenberger attempted to become the first to reach Hawaii by air nonstop from the mainland. Shortly after Maitland and Hegenberger left Oakland, California, in their Fokker C-3 trimotor, nicknamed "Bird of Paradise," they encountered trouble. The experimental radio-direction finder that was supposed to guide them safely to the islands stopped working. Despite this setback, the adventurers flew onward into the dark Pacific. They assumed their finely honed navigational skills would enable them to safely reach Hawaii some 2,500 miles from the mainland, but they would have little margin for error. Should they miss the islands, they would soon run out of gas and be forced to ditch the trimotor in the ocean, and, likely as not, they would never be seen again.

The trimotor engine droned on for nearly twenty-four hours, and the two men began to fear they had indeed flown past the archipelago. What could they do but strain their eyes for any sign of the islands? Then, Maitland saw what he thought was a flash of light. Without hesitation he turned toward it. The light proved to be the beacon of the Kilauea Point Light-

Once vital to mariners, the Kilauea Point Lighthouse now serves mostly as a tourist attraction.

(Courtesy Bob and Sandra Shanklin)

house on Kauai at the far northwestern end of the main island chain. About an hour later the "Bird of Paradise" landed at Wheeler Field on Oahu.

HOW TO GET THERE: *Kilauea Point National Wildlife Refuge and its lighthouse are located about ten miles northwest of Anahola off Highway 56 on Kauai. Call (808) 828–1413.*

Overnight guests at East Brother Light can enjoy unobstructed views of San Francisco Bay. The lighthouse/inn stands on a tiny island off San Pablo Point.

BIBLIOGRAPHY

Adams, William Henry Davenport. *Lighthouses and Lightships: A Descriptive and Historical Account of Their Mode of Construction and Organization.* New York: Scribner's, 1870.

Gibbs, Jim. *Lighthouses of the Pacific.* West Chester, Pa.: Schiffer Publishing Ltd., 1986.

Holland, Francis Ross, Jr. *America's Lighthouses: Their Illustrated History Since 1716.* Brattleboro, Vt.: Stephen Greene Press, 1972.

_____. *Great American Lighthouses.* Washington, D.C.: The Preservation Press, 1989.

Marx, Robert. *Shipwrecks of the Western Hemisphere.* New York: David McKay Company, 1971.

McCormick, William Henry. *The Modern Book of Lighthouses, Lifeboats, and Lightships.* London: W. Heinemann, 1913.

Moe, Christine. *Lighthouses and Lightships.* Monticello, Ill.: 1979.

Scheina, Robert L. "The Evolution of the Lighthouse Tower," *Lighthouses Then and Now* (supplement to the U.S. Coast Guard Commandant's Bulletin).

Shelton-Roberts, Cheryl and Bruce Roberts. *Lighthouse Families.* Birmingham, AL.: Crane Hill Publishers, 1997.

Snow, Edward Rowe. *Famous Lighthouses of America.* New York: Dodd, Mead, 1955.

_____. *Great Gales and Disasters.* New York: Dodd, Mead, 1952.

United States Coast Guard. *Historically Famous Lighthouses.* CG-232, 1986.

PHOTO INFORMATION

T‍he photographs in this book were taken on Fuji chrome color film and T-MAX black-and-white film. Other films, I'm sure, would have worked just as well; but being a travel photographer who takes trips constantly, I've learned to simplify what I take in my camera bag. The typical contents include two Nikon 8008 camera bodies with a small assortment of lenses: a 24-mm wide angle, a 35-135-mm zoom, a short telephoto lens such as an f2 85 mm, and a longer 70-300-mm zoom. Then there's my tripod; *yes, tripod.* When I was a young newspaper photographer, I thought tripods were for novice photographers who were afraid to blur images. Now I think only the overconfident do *not* use them. And for lighthouses, a tripod is a necessity unless you want only full-daylight pictures. In addition, there are in my camera case two little pieces of glass that I'm always looking for, and one or the other will be on my camera lens most of the time when I am shooting. One is a polarizing filter that enhances the color in bright, sunlit shots; the other is a warming filter that prevents the bluish cast that occurs on cloudy days and in deep shade on sunny days.

The photograph of Old Point Loma on page iii exemplifies the effect of a polarizing filter. The deep-blue sky and rich color have been enhanced by the filter. It is easy to use; place it on the lens and rotate it until the color looks best. The camera meter automatically adjusts the exposure.

There are two light shows, sunrise and dusk, at every lighthouse each day; these are the coveted times I like to be shooting. At most working lighthouses the light comes on half an hour before sunset and stays on for half an hour after sunrise, giving photographers an opportunity to work with the beacon's light shining. See the Crescent City photo on page 12 for an example. Also look at the East Brother Light on page 41. This is the effect of late-evening photography.

When photographing lighthouses, look for details such as the stairways, doorways, cornerstone dates, and windows, which all make good detail shots. At lighthouses where you can tour inside, objects and artifacts such as a coffeepot and cup add interest, or the light itself as exemplified in the photo of Point Arena Light on page 23.

A lighthouse's beam of light will look brighter if you can get a high elevation with your camera. Remember, the Fresnel lens is concentrating the light into a narrow beam; if you are standing at the base of the light, that beam is far above your head. Back off several hundred feet; the light will look a great deal more intense.

Try walking around the lighthouse, if possible, and viewing it from *all* the compass points. You may like one of the less-photographed points of view better than the usual angle. Remember, there is no "right" and "wrong" way to photograph a lighthouse. It's your film and imagination. Do it any way you like.

—Bruce Roberts

ABOUT THE AUTHORS

BRUCE ROBERTS and RAY JONES are the authors of *American Lighthouses* and eight books in Globe Pequot's colorful Lighthouses Series, including regional guides to New England, the Mid-Atlantic, the South, the Gulf Coast, the Eastern Great Lakes, the Western Great Lakes, the Pacific Northwest, and California and Hawaii.

BRUCE ROBERTS is a freelance photographer whose work has appeared in *Life, Sports Illustrated,* and Time-Life Books, and he has served as director of photography at *Southern Living* magazine. He is the recipient of many photography awards, and some of his photos are in the permanent collection of the Smithsonian Institution. Bruce and his wife, Cheryl, who helped with the research for this book, live on North Carolina's Outer Banks, not far from the Cape Lookout Island Lighthouse. In 1994 they founded the Outer Banks Lighthouse Society, and in 2000 they were recognized by the American Lighthouse Foundation and presented with the "Keeper of the Light" award for their work in lighthouse preservation.

RAY JONES is a freelance writer and publishing consultant who lives in Pebble Beach, California. In addition to his collaboration with Bruce Roberts, he is the co-author of several national lighthouse books, including *Lost Lighthouses, Endangered Lighthouses,* and *The Golden Age of American Lighthouses* as well as *Legendary Lighthouses* and *Legendary Lighthouses Volume II,* companions to the popular PBS series. He has served as an editor at Time-Life Books, as founding editor at *Albuquerque Living* magazine, as senior editor and writing coach at *Southern Living* magazine, and as founder and publisher of Country Roads Press.

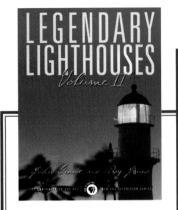
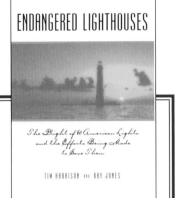
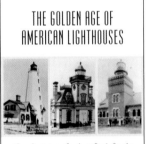
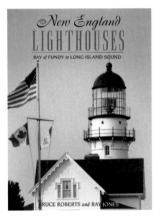
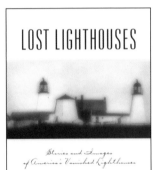